From the author of the #1 *Wall Street Journal* bestseller
StrengthsFinder 2.0

WELL BEING

The Five Essential Elements

TOM RATH
JIM HARTER

To Ashley and Harper, the source of my daily wellbeing.

-TR

To Laurie Dean (1966-2009). Inspiring Community Wellbeing.

-JH

GALLUP PRESS
1251 Avenue of the Americas
23rd Floor
New York, NY 10020

Library of Congress Control Number: 2010921093
ISBN: 978-1-59562-040-8

First Printing: 2010
10 9 8 7 6 5

Table of Contents

Your Wellbeing

Much of what we *think* will improve our wellbeing is either misguided or just plain wrong.

Contrary to what many people believe, wellbeing isn't just about being happy. Nor is it only about being wealthy or successful. And it's certainly not limited to physical health and wellness. In fact, focusing on any of these elements in isolation could drive us to feelings of frustration and even failure.

We are quick to buy into programs that promise to help us make money, lose weight, or strengthen our relationships. Then we spend the next few weeks dedicating our time and energy to that specific plan. Eventually, we give up on these programs when they conflict with other aspects of our lives.

If you've purchased books, watched videos, or attended classes on topics like these, you might have noticed how an intense focus on one area can actually be detrimental to your overall wellbeing. Just think of how many people dedicate an excessive amount of time and energy to their job at the expense of their personal relationships. It might seem easier to treat the critical areas in our lives as if they are independent and unrelated, but they're not. They are *interdependent*.

Wellbeing is about the combination of our love for what we do each day, the quality of our relationships, the security of our finances, the vibrancy of our physical health, and the pride we take in what we have contributed to our communities. Most importantly, it's about how these five elements *interact*.

What Makes Life Worthwhile

Gallup scientists have been exploring the demands of a life well-lived since the mid-20th century. More recently, in partnership with leading economists, psychologists, and other acclaimed scientists, we began to explore the common elements of wellbeing that transcend countries and cultures.

As part of this research, Gallup conducted a comprehensive global study of more than 150 countries, giving us a lens into the wellbeing of more than 98% of the world's population. From Afghanistan to Zimbabwe, we asked hundreds of questions about health, wealth, relationships, jobs, and communities. We then compared these results to how people experience their days and evaluate their lives overall.

In our initial research, we asked people what "the best possible future" for them would look like. We found that when evaluating their lives, people often give disproportionate weight to income and health: Across the groups we surveyed, "good health" and "wealth" were two of the most common responses. Perhaps this is because these things are easy to measure and track over time — we can monitor our height, weight, blood pressure, and household income. Yet we do not have a standard way to measure the quality of our careers or the health of our relationships.

So to construct a comprehensive measure of individual wellbeing, Gallup designed an assessment composed of the best questions we have asked over the last 50 years. To create this assessment, the Wellbeing Finder, we tested hundreds of questions across countries, languages, and vastly different life situations.

Upon completion of the research, five distinct statistical factors emerged. These are the universal elements of wellbeing that differentiate a thriving life from one spent suffering. They describe aspects of our lives that we can *do something about* and that are important to people in every situation we studied.

The Five Essential Elements

These elements are the currency of a life that matters. They do not include every nuance of what's important in life, but they do represent five broad categories that are essential to most people.

The first element is about how you occupy your time or simply liking what you do every day: your **Career Wellbeing**.

The second element is about having strong relationships and love in your life: your **Social Wellbeing**.

The third element is about effectively managing your economic life: your **Financial Wellbeing**.

The fourth element is about having good health and enough energy to get things done on a daily basis: your **Physical Wellbeing**.

The fifth element is about the sense of engagement you have with the area where you live: your **Community Wellbeing**.

While 66% of people are doing well in at least one of these areas, *just 7% are thriving in all five.* If we're struggling in any one of these domains, as most of us are, it damages our wellbeing and wears on our daily life. When we strengthen our wellbeing in any of these areas, we will have better days, months, and decades. But we're not getting the most out of our lives unless we're living effectively in all five.

Although these elements are universal across faiths, cultures, and nationalities, people take different paths to increasing their individual wellbeing. For many people, spirituality drives them in *all* these areas. Their faith is the most important facet of their lives, and it is the foundation of their daily efforts. For others, a deep mission, such as protecting the environment, inspires them each day. While the things that motivate us differ greatly from one person to the next, the outcomes do not.

There are many ways to create thriving Career, Social, Financial, Physical, and Community Wellbeing. Because these critical elements are within our control, we have the ability to improve them (for example, exercising, spending more time with friends, or using money wisely). However, the single biggest threat to our own wellbeing tends to be *ourselves*. Without even giving it much thought, we allow our short-term decisions to override what's best for our long-term wellbeing.

Working *Against* Our Own Best Interests

We know that physical activity will improve our health, yet we skip exercising. Missing one workout won't give us a heart attack or cause a stroke — so we let ourselves off the hook for a day.

We know that too much sugar and fried foods are bad for our health. But we grab a handful of candy or chips without even thinking. One french fry can't cause diabetes or obesity, right?

Similarly, we know it's important to spend quality time with our friends and family, but when work is pressing, we don't stop to ask a friend how he is doing.

When we think about our personal finances, we often spend instead of saving. Putting money into a retirement plan would yield several times its original value later on, but spending it on an indulgent purchase is so much more appealing right now.

With so many options to satisfy ourselves in the moment, it can be difficult to make the right long-term decisions. It is, after all, in our nature to do things that will provide the most immediate reward. This is wired into our DNA for basic survival. For decades, psychologists have described increases in the ability to delay gratification as a cornerstone of human development from childhood to adulthood.

But the reality is, our short-term self still wins and gets dessert, despite objections from our long-term self that wants a healthy body and a long life. For example, when we asked more than 23,000 people about their purchasing habits, only 10% said that they buy candy regularly. But when we asked the same group of people later in the survey if there was a bowl of candy sitting right in front of them if they would eat some, more than 70% admitted they would.

As long as we allow short-term desires to win, it will be difficult to effect long-term behavioral change. However, we learned from people with the highest levels of wellbeing that there is a simple solution to this problem: If we can find *short-term incentives that are consistent with our long-term objectives*, it is much easier to make the right decisions in the moment.

For example, we're more likely to skip a cheeseburger and fries not when we ponder the long-term risk of obesity or diabetes, but when we consider the short-term reality that devouring it will lead to a "high-fat hangover" that ruins *the rest of the day*. Or we might choose to exercise tomorrow morning because we know that just 20 minutes of activity can boost our mood for the next 12 hours.

When we can see an immediate payoff, we are more likely to change our behavior *in the moment*. This aligns our daily actions with our long-term interests. So wanting more energy throughout the day (short-term incentive) leads to exercising

20 minutes each morning (a better decision in the moment), and this eventually leads to avoiding chronic health issues (the long-term objective). As we will discuss throughout the book, setting these "positive defaults" and making even small changes to our daily routines can have a major and lasting impact on our wellbeing.

Thriving Wellbeing

In the sections that follow, we refer to people we interviewed who have thriving wellbeing in each of the five elements. These people had the highest levels of wellbeing in our entire database. As we learned from those who are thriving, improving wellbeing in any one of the five areas takes work and accountability. But we hope that after reading this book, you will have a more holistic view of what contributes to your wellbeing over a lifetime. This will enable you to enjoy each day, get more out of life in general, and perhaps most importantly, boost the wellbeing of your friends, family members, colleagues, and others in your community.

1: Career Wellbeing

Do you like what you do each day?

This might be the most basic, yet important, wellbeing question we can ask ourselves. Yet only 20% of people can give a strong "yes" in response.

At a fundamental level, we all need something to do, and ideally something to look forward to, when we wake up every day. What you spend your time doing each day shapes your identity, whether you are a student, parent, volunteer, retiree, or have a more conventional job.

We spend the majority of our waking hours during the week doing something we consider a career, occupation, vocation, or job. When people first meet, they ask each other, "What do you *do?*" If your answer to that question is something you find fulfilling and meaningful, you are likely thriving in Career Wellbeing.

People usually underestimate the influence of their career on their overall wellbeing. But Career Wellbeing is arguably the most essential of the five elements. If you don't have the opportunity to regularly do something you enjoy — even if it's more of a passion or interest than something you get paid to do — the odds of your having high wellbeing in other areas diminish rapidly. People with high Career Wellbeing are more than *twice* as likely to be thriving in their lives overall.

Imagine that you have great social relationships, financial security, and good physical health — but you don't like what you do every day. Chances are, much of your social time is spent worrying or complaining about your lousy job. And this causes stress, taking a toll on your physical health. If your Career Wellbeing is low, it's easy to see how it can cause deterioration in other areas over time.

Losing Your Identity

To appreciate how much our careers shape our identity and wellbeing, consider what happens when someone loses a job and remains unemployed for a full year. A landmark study published in *The Economic Journal* revealed that unemployment might be the only major life event from which people do not fully recover within five years. This study followed 130,000 people for several decades, allowing researchers to look at the way major life events such as marriage, divorce, birth of a child, or death of a spouse affect our life satisfaction over time.

One of the more encouraging findings was that, even in the face of some of life's most tragic events like the death of a spouse, after a few years, people *do* recover to the same level of wellbeing they had before their spouse passed away. But this was not the case for those who were unemployed for a prolonged period of time — particularly not for men. *Our wellbeing actually recovers more rapidly from the death of a spouse than it does from a sustained period of unemployment.*

The Impact on Wellbeing
In the years before and after the event

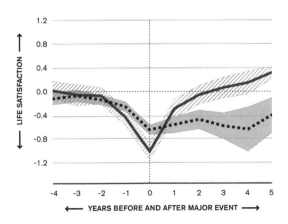

Adapted from Clark, et al., *The Economic Journal*, June 2008

This doesn't mean that getting fired will harm your wellbeing forever. The same study also found that being laid off from a job in the last year did *not* result in any significant long-term changes. The key is to avoid sustained periods of unemployment (more than a year) when you are actively looking for a job but unable to find one. In addition to the obvious loss of income from prolonged unemployment, the lack of regular social contact and the daily boredom might be even more detrimental to your wellbeing.

You don't need to earn a paycheck to have thriving Career Wellbeing. But you do need to find something that you enjoy doing — and have an opportunity to do it every day. Whether that means working in an office, volunteering, raising your children, or starting your own business, what matters most is being engaged in the career or occupation you choose.

Waiting for the Bell to Ring

Think back to when you were in school sitting through a class in which you had very little interest. Perhaps your eyes were fixed on the clock or you were staring blankly into space. You probably remember the anticipation of waiting for the bell to ring so you could get up from your desk and move on to whatever was next. More than two-thirds of workers around the world experience a similar feeling by the end of a typical workday.

To explore why so many people are disengaged at work, we recruited 168 employees and studied their engagement, heart rate, stress levels, and various emotions throughout the day. Before the study began, we collected data about each employee's level of engagement. We examined the differences between employees who were generally engaged in their jobs and those who were not. As part of the experiment, the participants carried a handheld device that alerted them at various points in the day when we would ask them what they were doing, who they were with, and several other questions about their mood.

We also asked each participant to wear a small heart rate monitor. At the end of each day, these monitors, which were smaller than a quarter and attached to the chest like a sticker, were connected to a computer to download data. This allowed us to study the relationship between fluctuations in heart rate and various events throughout the day.

Saliva samples were also collected to gauge stress levels throughout the day (via the stress hormone, cortisol). Whenever the handheld device beeped and requested an entry in the electronic journal, participants were asked to spit into a small tube. The cortisol levels in the saliva provided us with a direct physiological measure of stress levels at various points each day.

After reviewing all of these data, it was clear that when people who are engaged in their jobs show up for work, they have an *entirely different experience* than those who are disengaged. For those who were engaged, happiness and interest throughout the day were significantly higher. Conversely, stress levels were substantially higher for those who were disengaged. Perhaps most strikingly, disengaged workers' stress levels decreased and their happiness increased toward the end of the workday. As you can see from the following graphic, people with low engagement and low Career Wellbeing are simply waiting for the workday to end.

Engagement at Work and Happiness Throughout the Day

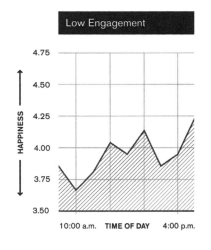
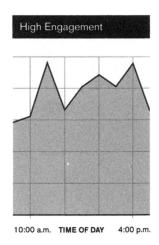

Enjoying Week*days* as Much as Week*ends*

As part of this same study, we explored the differences in momentary experiences between working and nonworking days. We found that engaged workers had similar happiness levels on working and nonworking days, with only slight increases in stress and a positive boost in interest levels when they were at work. However, disengaged workers experienced dramatic drops in happiness and interest — as well as major increases in stress — during working days.

For those who are engaged, a day at work might be slightly more stressful than the weekend, but that is offset by normal levels of happiness and even more interest when they are at work. However, disengaged workers live for the weekend and dread the workday. So if your Career Wellbeing is thriving, you are able to have good weekends *and* good weekdays, and the time you are at work is as enjoyable as the time you spend away from work.

As we learned from Jay, a mechanical engineer with thriving Career Wellbeing, enjoying what you do on a day-to-day basis is essential. Like many people, Jay has had several jobs over the span of his career, and at times, he has had to deal with frustrating office politics. Yet he stuck with his passion for managing engineering projects. This passion and interest helped him maintain high Career Wellbeing.

When we asked Jay about what interests him most, he described how much he likes learning about the mechanics of how things work. He enjoys the process of determining the thickness of the floor slabs, column spacing, and steel beams based on the height of a wall. Jay also brings his passion for work home — he is always remodeling his house. In his spare time, he researches foundation design and new methods for constructing buildings. This was one of the patterns we observed among people with thriving Career Wellbeing: They love their work so much that it is closely aligned with — and can't help but spill over into — their personal lives.

Are Bad Workplaces Killing People?

The extreme variation between a good weekend and a bad weekday might explain why heart attacks are more likely to occur on Mondays. This suggests a rough transition from Sunday to Monday that takes a physical toll. In the aforementioned study, we were able to examine how physiological stress (based on cortisol levels in the saliva samples we collected) fluctuates from workdays to weekends.

Cortisol is a stress hormone that boosts blood pressure and blood sugar levels while suppressing the immune system. It is essential for normal functioning, and some spikes in cortisol levels are necessary to trigger our fight-or-flight response when we are in danger. But often, we perceive situations to be more serious than they really are.

For example, if your boss criticizes your work, or if you are performing a task that is frustrating, your cortisol levels spike rapidly. When a burst of cortisol flushes through your system, blood starts to rush through your veins. Your heart rate goes up as you start to breathe faster. What you can feel on the inside, others may see on the outside as your pupils dilate or as sweat begins to bead on your forehead.

While activation of this fight-or-flight response serves us well in a real emergency, it is not as helpful in a traffic jam or a heated meeting at work. These are not life-or-death situations, but our brain doesn't know the difference. So when we transition from a leisurely Sunday, the least stressful day of the week, to Monday morning in a workplace where we are not engaged, it might damage our bodies in the process.

Work Alters the Brain and Bloodstream

Boosting Career Wellbeing might also reduce the risk of anxiety and depression. In 2008, we studied a large panel of randomly selected workers who agreed to be contacted regularly. We measured their engagement levels and asked them if they had ever been diagnosed with depression. We excluded those who reported that they had been diagnosed with depression from our analysis. When we contacted the remaining panel members in 2009, we again asked them if they had been diagnosed with depression in the last year.

It turned out that 5% of our panel members (who had no diagnosis of depression as of 2008) had been newly diagnosed with depression. Further, those who were actively disengaged in their careers in 2008 were nearly *twice as likely to be diagnosed with depression* over the next year. While there are many factors that contribute to depression, being disengaged at work appears to be a leading indicator of a subsequent clinical diagnosis of depression.

On a more encouraging note, as workers become more engaged, their physical health can improve in parallel. In another study, we tracked employees for two years to examine the relationship between changes in engagement at work and changes in cholesterol and triglyceride levels. We surveyed these workers about their engagement at work every six months, and we collected blood samples to measure their cholesterol and triglycerides each year.

As employees' levels of engagement at work increased, their total cholesterol and triglyceride levels significantly decreased. And those with decreasing levels of engagement at work had an increase in total cholesterol and triglycerides. These results suggest one possible mechanism through which our workplace experiences directly influence our physical health. Boosting your Career Wellbeing might be one of the most important priorities to consider for maintaining good health over the years.

Is a Good Boss as Important as a Good Doctor?

Behavioral scientists and economists have become increasingly interested in how people spend their time. Time-use studies provide important data about what people do with their time, who they spend it with, and how they feel at various points throughout the day. One of the major findings from this research is that the person we *least* enjoy being around is our boss.

Of all the categories people ranked, from friends to relatives to coworkers to children, they rated the time they spent with their manager as being the worst time of the day. Even when compared to a list of specific daily activities, time spent with one's boss was actually rated lower than time spent doing chores and cleaning the house. This helps explain why a study of more than 3,000 workers in Sweden found that those who deemed their managers to be the least competent had a 24% higher risk of a serious heart problem. For those who had worked for that manager for more than four years, the risk was 39% higher.

The most disengaged group of workers we have ever studied are those who have a manager who is simply not paying attention. If your manager ignores you, there is a 40% chance that you will be actively disengaged or filled with hostility about your job. If your manager is at least paying attention — even if he is focusing on your weaknesses — the chances of your being actively disengaged go down to 22%. *But if your manager is primarily focusing on your strengths, the chance of your being actively disengaged is just 1%, or 1 in 100.*

While most of us do not have the liberty to choose our boss, we often overlook the profound impact this relationship has on our engagement at work, our physical health, and our overall wellbeing. As one person with struggling Career Wellbeing put it, "When I discover a problem at work or bring an issue to my manager, no one listens. And then the quality of the product suffers. It's frustrating, because I want to do good work. If you take something to your supervisor and he doesn't listen or care, you begin to stop caring too." Clearly, people looking for a new job should be as concerned about who their manager will be as they are about their job title, their benefits, the company's reputation, or even the pay.

Using Your Strengths to Avoid Burnout

So many lives — and in some cases, entire cultures — are built around the premise that work is something we are *not* supposed to enjoy. This fundamentally flawed perception is woven into societies and economic models around the world. As a result, people strive to minimize the number of hours they need to work in a day or week, and they try to retire as early as possible. Then paradoxically, as they near "retirement age," they realize how dull life would be if they were not working at all. According to one study, by the time people reach their 50s, nearly two-thirds *want* to keep working.

A 1958 study conducted by the late George Gallup found that Career Wellbeing is one of the major differentiators that helps us live into our 90s. As part of this classic "old age study," Gallup conducted in-depth interviews with hundreds of Americans who were 95 and older. While the standard retirement age for men in the 1950s was closer to 65, men who lived to see 95 did not retire until they were *80 years old* on average. Even more remarkable, 93% of these men reported getting a great deal of satisfaction out of the work they did, and 86% reported having *fun* doing their job.

One of the essentials to having fun at work is getting the opportunity to use your strengths every day. When we build on our strengths and daily successes — instead of focusing on failures — we simply learn more. Compared to those who do *not* get to focus on what they do best, people who have the opportunity to use their strengths are *six times* as likely to be engaged in their jobs and more than *three times* as likely to report having an excellent quality of life. Our global data show that these people can enjoy a full 40-hour workweek, while those who *do not* get to use their strengths get burned out after just 20 hours of work per week.

By no means are you immune from getting exhausted and stressed out — even if you have a job you love. Consistently working more than 60 hours a week is probably a bad idea, no matter how much you enjoy what you do. But people who want or need to work more than 20 hours a week better find a job that fits their strengths.

The Essentials of Career Wellbeing

People with high Career Wellbeing wake up every morning with something to look forward to doing that day. Whether they are working in a home, a classroom, or a cubicle, they have the opportunity to use their strengths each day and to make progress. Those with thriving Career Wellbeing have a deep purpose in life and a plan to attain their goals. In most cases, they have a leader or manager who makes them enthusiastic about the future and friends who share their passion.

While you might think that people with high Career Wellbeing spend too much time working, they actually take *more* time to enjoy life, have better relationships, and don't take things for granted. And they love what they do each day.

Three Recommendations for Boosting Career Wellbeing:

1. Every day, use your strengths.

2. Identify someone with a shared mission who encourages your growth. Spend more time with this person.

3. Opt into more social time with the people and teams you enjoy being around at work.

2: Social Wellbeing

When you reflect on the most memorable events, experiences, and moments in your life, you'll notice that they have something in common: the presence of another person. The best moments — and most agonizing ones — occur at the intersection between two people. Yet we often underestimate the impact of our closest relationships and social connections.

Scientists are discovering how relationships shape our expectations, desires, and goals. Emotions spread quickly from one person to the next. When you see a friend who is happy, this often causes you to smile, and as a result, you feel better. Or if you have a frustrating meeting late in the day, your emotional state is likely to transfer to your spouse when you get home. Because we tend to synchronize our moods with the people around us, our emotions influence one another throughout the day.

Do We Inherit More From Friends Than From Family?

Not only do the people directly around us influence our wellbeing, so does our friends' independent network of relationships. According to a Harvard study, our wellbeing is dependent on our *entire network*. This research, which was based on a 30+ year longitudinal study of more than 12,000 people who were all part of one interconnected network, found that your odds of being happy increase by 15% if a direct connection in your social network is happy. In other words, having direct and frequent social contact with someone who has high wellbeing dramatically boosts your chances of being happy.

Even more critical is the degree to which *indirect* connections influence our wellbeing. The Harvard study found a similar effect for secondhand associations. So if a friend of your direct connection is happy, the odds of your friend being happy increase by 15% — and the odds of *you* being happy increase by 10% even if you don't know or interact with this secondhand connection.

Even your friend's friend's friend influences your wellbeing. According to this massive study of social networks, you are 6% more likely to be happy if a connection three degrees removed from you is happy. While a 6% increase in happiness might not seem that significant, it actually is when compared to the effect of having a higher income. According to this research, an increase of about $10,000 in annual income was associated with just a 2% increased likelihood of being happy. This led the study's authors to conclude that the wellbeing of friends and relatives is a more effective predictor of happiness than earning more money. As Harvard researcher Nicholas Christakis summarized: "People are embedded in social networks and the health and wellbeing of one person affects the health and wellbeing of others. . . . Human happiness is not merely the province of isolated individuals."

Christakis has also explored how our social connections influence our habits, behaviors, and health. When it comes to smoking, you are 61% more likely to smoke if you have a direct connection with a smoker (compared with the likelihood based on chance). At the second degree of separation, you're still 29% more likely to smoke if your friend's friend is a smoker. And at the third degree, you are 11% more likely to smoke.

In this context, it's easy to see how peer pressure has cut smoking rates in half over the last few decades. As smoking becomes less acceptable in one social circle (e.g., a workplace), it quickly spreads to related networks of friends and family members. Over the span of this study, smokers were essentially pushed out to the edges of the network between 1971 and 2000.

Secondhand Obesity

Our social circles have a direct impact on our weight as well. If a friend of yours becomes obese, it increases your chances of becoming obese by 57%. If your brother or sister becomes obese, it boosts your chances of being obese by 40%. And if your spouse becomes obese, the odds of your becoming obese go up by 37%.

Over time, our diets and exercise habits mimic those of our friends. If your best friend is very active, it nearly *triples* your chances of having high levels of physical activity. We found that people with a best friend who has a very healthy diet are more than *five times as likely* to have a very healthy diet as well. Your best friend's diet is an even stronger predictor of whether you have a healthy diet than the dietary habits of your parents. So the people we surround ourselves with might have more influence on our health than our family history does.

Combining social interaction with physical activity has a compounding effect on our wellbeing. Kelly, a teacher who has some of the highest levels of Social Wellbeing *and* Physical Wellbeing we saw, illustrated how integral her friendships are to her physical health.

Kelly's husband, who wakes up every morning and goes to the gym, always pushes her to be more active. They spend a good deal of time exercising outdoors. But it is her friend Lisa who really keeps her going on a daily basis. Every morning, they meet at Kelly's house and walk at least four miles. This is how they hold each other accountable — they have to show up for the other person. Kelly admitted that the only time she gets "a little lazy" is when Lisa is out of town.

Kelly also gets more involved in an exercise routine when she's with someone. She thrives on the camaraderie, going to parks, and getting outdoors. "If I'm alone, it's a burden," she said. "I'll even get up earlier if I know Lisa is out of town just to get it over with. I look at it at that point like a job. I know it's good for me, so I do it and get it over with. And I'm always happy I did it." But it's not the same as when she is with a friend and "time flies." Kelly described how much better she feels throughout the day because of the time she spent exercising with friends.

We Have Stock in Others' Wellbeing

There is something about having close friendships in general that is good for our physiological health. Relationships serve as a buffer during tough times, which in turn improves our cardiovascular functioning and decreases stress levels. On the other hand, people with very few social ties have nearly twice the risk of dying from heart disease and are twice as likely to catch colds — even though they are less likely to have the exposure to germs that comes from frequent social contact.

To study how one of our closest relationships influences our physical health, a team of researchers designed a clever experiment in which they studied how stress levels affect the time it takes to recover from a wound. The researchers brought 42 married couples into a hospital and created several small wounds on their arms. They then placed devices over the wounds to measure the rate of healing.

The results revealed that it took almost *twice as long for the wounds to heal* for couples who reported having hostility in their relationship. So if you're in a strained relationship, it could extend the time it takes for you to recover from surgery or a major injury. As scientists continue to explore the connection between our relationships and our health, they are discovering that our Social Wellbeing might have *even more influence on how quickly we recover* than conventional risk factors.

Another implication from this research is that *proximity matters*. A friend who lives within a mile of you will likely have more influence on your wellbeing than a friend who lives several miles away. Even your next-door neighbor's wellbeing has an impact on yours.

Because your entire social network affects your health, habits, and wellbeing, mutual friendships matter even more. These are relationships in which you and one of your close friends share a friendship with a third person. Investing in these mutual relationships will lead to even higher levels of wellbeing. This is why it is critical for us to do what we can to strengthen the *entire* network around us. Simply put, we have stock in others' wellbeing.

Every Hour of Social Time Keeps Stress Away

In addition to close relationships and proximity, the sheer amount of time we spend socializing matters. The data suggest that to have a thriving day, we need *six hours* of social time. When we get at least six hours of daily social time, it increases our wellbeing and minimizes stress and worry. Just so you don't think that six hours of social time is unattainable in one day, it's important to note that the six hours includes time at work, at home, on the telephone, talking to friends, sending e-mail, and other communication.

When people have almost no social time in a given day, they have an equal chance of having a good day or a bad day. However, *each hour of social time quickly decreases the odds of having a bad day*. Even three hours of social time reduces the chances of having a bad day to 10%. And each additional hour of social time — up to about six hours — improves the odds of having a good day.

While six hours of social time in one day might seem like a lot, people with thriving Social Wellbeing *average* about six hours a day. Even when we studied subgroups of people with various personality types (from outgoing to introverted) and compared weekdays to weekends, each additional hour of social time in a day had a measureable benefit.

Beyond the immediate increase in wellbeing that comes with each hour of social time, the long-term benefits can be even more profound, particularly as we age. A study of more than 15,000 people over the age of 50 found that among those who were socially active, their memories declined at *less than half the rate* compared to those who were the least social.

Without a Friend, Work Is a Lonely Place

Gallup has conducted extensive studies on the value of friendships in the workplace. One of the most revealing questions we have asked more than 15 million employees all over the world is whether they have a "best friend at work." We use this very specific wording because early research indicated that having a "best friend" at work was a more powerful predictor of workplace outcomes than simply having a "friend" or even a "good friend."

Our research revealed that just 30% of employees have a best friend at work. Those who do are *seven times* as likely to be engaged in their jobs, are better at engaging customers, produce higher quality work, have higher wellbeing, and are less likely to get injured on the job. In sharp contrast, those without a best friend in the workplace have just a *1 in 12* chance of being engaged.

What is it about a close friendship in the workplace that makes such a profound difference? To find out, we examined what momentary experiences throughout the course of a day lead to higher wellbeing and engagement. We discovered that the single best predictor is not *what* people are doing — but *who* they are with.

It doesn't even matter if two friends at work are engaged in tasks that are directly related to workplace productivity. According to a study conducted by a team of MIT researchers in which workers wore high-tech identity badges throughout the day that monitored their movements and conversations, idle chit-chat might actually be valuable to productivity. The researchers found that even small increases in social cohesiveness lead to large gains in production.

If you don't work in an office building filled with people and places to congregate, it's still possible to develop close relationships. Roland, a project manager with thriving Social Wellbeing explained: "The three people I work with most are scattered across the country, and we only see each other in person a couple times per year. But it is rare that a day or even a weekend passes when we are not discussing politics or sports via e-mail." The most progressive organizations realize how technology can enable not just work-related tasks, but also help workers stay personally connected.

Don't Expect One Friend to Do It All

Social Wellbeing starts with having at least one close friendship. What's more, the *quality* of that relationship plays an extremely important role in your overall health and wellbeing. One study revealed that marital strain actually accelerates the decline in our physical health as we age.

Each additional close friendship you have contributes even more to your life and daily experiences. Our research has found that people who have at least three or four very close friendships are healthier, have higher wellbeing, and are more engaged in their jobs. But the absence of any close friendships can lead to boredom, loneliness, and depression.

The Harvard research on social networks revealed that, while each happy friend increases your odds of being happy by about 9%, each unhappy friend only decreases your odds of being happy by 7%. This might explain why, on average, each new relationship is likely to boost your wellbeing.

Scott, who has thriving Social Wellbeing, described how each of his closest relationships makes a unique contribution to his life. His father always asks him good questions and motivates him in his career. His wife helps him be more socially involved than he would be on his own. Scott also has a tightly knit group of colleagues he spends time with every day. They come together to help one another through financial problems, relationship issues, conflicts at work, and personal health challenges.

Instead of expecting one person to fulfill all his needs and setting that relationship up for failure, Scott relies on the strengths of his network. More than 80% of the people we studied report that they contribute something very different than they receive from their closest friendship. So the key to great relationships is to focus on what each friend *does* contribute, instead of expecting one person to do it all.

The Essentials of Social Wellbeing

People with thriving Social Wellbeing have several close relationships that help them achieve, enjoy life, and be healthy. They are surrounded by people who encourage their development and growth. Those with high Social Wellbeing deliberately spend time — on average about six hours a day — investing in their social networks. They make time for gatherings and trips that strengthen these relationships even more. As a result, people with thriving Social Wellbeing have great relationships, which gives them positive energy on a daily basis.

Three Recommendations for Boosting Social Wellbeing:

1. Spend six hours a day socializing with friends, family, and colleagues (this time includes work, home, phone, e-mail, and other communication).

2. Strengthen the mutual connections in your network.

3. Mix social time with physical activity. For example, take a long walk with a friend so you can motivate each other to be healthy.

3: Financial Wellbeing

As we studied a great deal of research on the topic of money and its importance in our lives, what we found challenged many of our assumptions. Advice from personal finance gurus wasn't holding up. Nor, frankly, was a central tenet of classic economics, in which the assumption is that people make rational decisions that result in optimal monetary gain. Most strikingly, we learned that the amount of money you have — the gold standard of measuring financial health — is not the best gauge of your Financial Wellbeing, let alone your life in general.

Do You Need Money to Be Happy?

Many books and articles assert that money is not that important to our overall happiness. When making this claim, the authors usually mention research showing that people who won the lottery were not much happier several years later. Others cite studies showing that income matters only up to the point at which people have enough money to afford their basic needs. And the media have endless stories about wealthy people who are otherwise miserable.

It would be nice to believe that we all have the same opportunity to be happy, regardless of our income level. But our data suggest that this is false. Based on a comprehensive study using Gallup wellbeing data from 132 countries, there is undoubtedly a relationship between wellbeing and Gross Domestic Product (GDP) per capita — and the connection is much stronger than we would have guessed. Clearly, wealthier countries have citizens with higher wellbeing. So although money doesn't guarantee happiness, being in a wealthy country certainly increases your odds of having a good life.

The Economics of Wellbeing

People in wealthier nations have higher evaluations of their lives overall

● Population (bigger circles = larger countries)

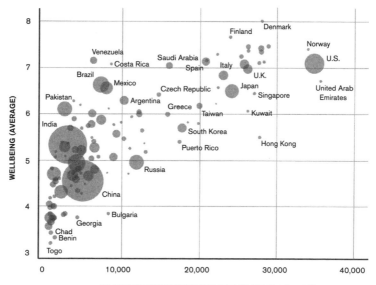

ECONOMIC OUTPUT (GDP) PER PERSON (IN U.S. DOLLARS)

Gallup global research using the Cantril Self-Anchoring Striving Scale

At the risk of stating the obvious, money is valuable because it buys food for people and their families and puts a roof over their heads. Like the wide range of wealth and poverty across countries, average wellbeing also varies widely from Togo to Denmark. This variation is due in large part to differences in access to basics like food, shelter, and safety from extreme violence. For example, across Africa, 56% of people we studied reported that there were times when their family had "gone hungry" in the last 12 months.

In lower income countries, pain is one of the leading causes of suffering. And having the money to pay for basic healthcare can improve wellbeing through the alleviation of physical pain. So for a great number of people around the world, money is absolutely essential for meeting basic needs.

In middle to higher income countries, the differences in wellbeing levels can be explained by the daily enjoyment and comfort afforded by money. Generally, those who have a lot of money can do *what* they want *when* they want to do it. Money can increase short-term happiness by giving us more control over how we spend our time, whether that means a shorter commute, more time at home with family, or additional social time with friends.

How You *Can* Buy Wellbeing

When a team of Harvard researchers surveyed people about their spending on themselves, their spending on others, and their happiness, they found that spending on oneself does *not* boost wellbeing. However, spending money on others does — and it appears to be as important to people's happiness as the total amount of money they make.

In another experiment, the same investigators studied people who had recently received a large sum of "bonus" money from their organization's profit-sharing program and tracked how each person chose to spend this money. As you might expect, some people spent their money on personal items such as bills, expenses, rent, mortgage, or material goods. Others spent the extra money on something for another person or donated the money to charity. Again, spending money on oneself didn't boost happiness, while spending the money on others did.

In a third experiment, the researchers tracked individuals throughout the course of a single day. Each study participant received an envelope containing either $5 or $20 and was asked to spend all the money by 5:00 that day. Participants were randomly assigned to either spend the money on personal items, to use it to buy a gift for someone else, or to give it to charity. The amount of money the participants were given had no relationship to their levels of happiness at the end of the day. It was *how* the money was spent that mattered. Once again, the participants who spent the money on a gift for someone else or who gave it to charity experienced a significant boost in wellbeing by the end of the day, while people who spent the money on themselves did not.

Turning to Retail Therapy

When we are feeling down, trying to cheer ourselves up by going on a personal shopping spree is unlikely to help in the long run. Sadness may even lead us to spend *a lot more* money on ourselves than we otherwise would. People who were shown a video designed to induce sadness offered to pay *nearly four times as much* for a product when compared with a group that did not watch the video. Despite this major difference, people in the "sadness" group insisted that the video's sad content had *not* influenced their decision.

Even though we don't realize it, a bad mood could lead to a cascade of poor financial decisions. While spending on ourselves isn't likely to help much, this research suggests that the worst time to make a major purchase is when you are feeling down. We spend the *most* when we feel the *worst*. So much for "retail therapy."

Spending on Experiences and Memories

Buying *experiences* such as going out to dinner or taking a vacation increases our own wellbeing and the wellbeing of others. Experiences last while material purchases fade. Even if you feel better immediately after your purchase, studies show that our satisfaction with material goods decreases over time.

But if we use our money to buy pleasant experiences, we get the benefit of looking forward to the event, the actual experience, and in some cases, decades of fond memories. Material items lose their novelty, but *we can relive memories indefinitely*. Even brief experiential purchases such as dining out or going to a movie increase our wellbeing. In addition to satisfying our need for social time, we are less likely to regret experiential purchases, which increases our satisfaction with these decisions over time.

One of the people we interviewed with thriving Financial Wellbeing, Susan, is quite frugal in managing her family's money, and she avoids unnecessary purchases. But she and her husband make a point of spending money on fun and memorable experiences such as taking their granddaughter to see a movie. They have also saved money for trips with friends. When we talked with Susan, she and her husband were planning a cruise with another couple. "We've been on vacation with them twice, and we have a really good time together," she said. "So when we told them we were going on a cruise, they said they would go too." When Susan describes the way she spends money, she is mindful about spending on social events instead of focusing on material possessions.

Because spending on experiences boosts our spirits for the long term, it explains part of the connection between money and wellbeing. For those who make less than $25,000 a year, experiential and material purchases produce similar gains in wellbeing. However, as income levels increase, experiential purchases produce *two to three times* the levels of wellbeing when compared to material purchases.

We don't get bored with fond memories like we do with tangible objects. And we don't second-guess whether we should have made a different decision, as we do with material things. When we purchase meaningful experiences, it buys us memories that continue to grow, and we get more out of every dollar we spend.

The Comparison Dilemma

For years, traditional economists have assumed that people make rational decisions that are in their best interests. But the relatively new discipline of behavioral economics is proving otherwise. Consider the following two scenarios, and assuming the same purchasing power in both, which one would you choose?

A. An annual income of $50,000, while the people around you earn $25,000 a year.

B. An annual income of $100,000, while the people around you earn $200,000 a year.

Using a classic economic model, everyone should choose an income of $100,000 over $50,000. Instead, nearly half the people presented with these options pick the lower salary of $50,000 a year. They choose to make *half* the total income as long as it is double the income of their peers. It seems that the amount of money we make or the size of our home is less relevant than how they compare to others' income and possessions. This plays out in the decisions we make every day, and that poses a real dilemma.

You might install a new deck on your house in the fall and be glowing with pride, only to see your neighbor install a bigger one in the spring. The reality is, we have a built-in need to compare ourselves to those around us, particularly when it comes to the most tangible or visible means. Yet as many people have learned, continuing to define ourselves by social comparison makes for a never-ending rat race. Boosting our Career Wellbeing and our Social Wellbeing is one way around this comparison dilemma.

Gallup asked a random sample of U.S. workers about how they perceive their pay and whether they think it is appropriate for the work they do. Most people think they should be getting paid more, which is not a big surprise. But that isn't what we were actually studying. We were measuring how engaged these people were in their jobs and how likely they were to leave their company in the next 12 months.

At the exact same levels of pay and job responsibilities, some people feel their pay is adequate, while others do not. The differences in how people perceive their pay are largely dependent on how engaged they are in their work. Those with high Career Wellbeing perceive the same amount of pay much more favorably than those with low Career Wellbeing do. Even when asked to compare themselves to the people they spend a lot of time with, those with thriving Career Wellbeing and thriving Social Wellbeing are nearly two times as likely to say they are satisfied with their standard of living.

Money is easily counted, but it is still a highly subjective variable in our lives. If you want to improve your Financial Wellbeing, first make sure that your Career Wellbeing and your Social Wellbeing are thriving. If your daily work is fulfilling and your relationships are strong, you are substantially less likely to get caught up in this comparison dilemma. And you won't be as tempted to keep up with the proverbial Joneses.

Using Irrationality to Your Advantage

Studies from the field of behavioral economics have exposed the irrationality of our financial decision making. But they also highlight how we can manage these inherent biases. Our mental accounting does not work logically like the cells in a spreadsheet. We are what scientists call "loss averse." In other words, it hurts a lot more to lose $50 that we already have than it feels good to win $50.

We view money in relative — not absolute — terms. The same $50 is interpreted differently depending on whether we're buying a car or paying for a meal, even though it is the same dollar amount. Finding $50 on the street will do more to boost our wellbeing than having $50 cut from our utility bill, even though the amount is the same.

These biases play out every day, even if we don't realize it. Perhaps the most common example of this is the use of credit cards, which takes the pain out of the loss associated with making a payment because we can defer it until later. As University of Chicago economist Richard Thaler describes, credit cards act as a "decoupling device" because they separate the joy of the immediate purchase from the pain of the payment, which is off in the distant future.

Credit card companies and marketers will always tempt our desire for immediate gratification, but modern technology also affords us the ability to set up automated systems that work to our advantage. We can have taxes, benefits, insurance, and retirement savings deducted directly from our paycheck. Then, when that virtual paycheck is automatically deposited into our bank account, we can set up systems to pay off previous commitments (mortgage, bills, car) and even set aside a specified amount or percentage for savings. This leaves us with a remainder that we can spend on the things we need and want *without* the burden of debt.

We often do not take the time to set the right "defaults" in the first place. Putting money into retirement savings, especially when it is tax-deferred, is a wise decision for long-term financial growth and stability. Yet most people won't participate in a retirement plan if they have to consciously opt in. Research has shown that when a company requires employees to explicitly opt in to a retirement plan, most workers do not participate. But when the default is for employees to be automatically enrolled, *more than 80% participate* in the retirement plan.

Setting Positive Defaults

There are lots of examples of how we can use positive defaults to our advantage. When we interviewed people with thriving Financial Wellbeing, a consistent but surprising pattern emerged. Generally, they were not "rich" by traditional measures. Yet they had enough money to meet their needs, and they rarely had to endure the stress of worrying about not being able to pay their bills.

Linda, a rural mail carrier, described how carefully managing her money leads to thriving Financial Wellbeing: "I get paid twice a month, and I live on one paycheck. And one paycheck I save. So if I make a dollar, I spend 45 cents, and I save 55 or 60 cents. So I always live below my means."

Linda has set up default systems to make sure that she adheres to this plan. One of her two paychecks each month is automatically deposited into a long-term savings account. She said, "Once (the money) is pulled, I don't see it. So since I don't see it, I know I only have this much (to spend)." Linda also set up the long-term account so that her brother has to sign with her to withdraw any money. These strategies ensure that she is not spending unnecessarily. Linda tracks her balance in the remaining account to evaluate her finances each month.

Linda and others with high Financial Wellbeing realize that they need to structure the right defaults in the short term (e.g., automated payroll deduction) to thrive financially in the long run. Instead of following the minimum defaults set by others, such as a lender or the government, they take control and assume responsibility for their financial future. This helps them decrease their debt and alleviate the stress and guilt that come with purchases made with loans or credit. As Linda put it, "If there's something I want, I'm secure enough that I can buy it and pay for it without feeling any guilt."

Is Wealth Accumulation the Wrong Target?

Income, debt, and net worth are some of the most common metrics we use to evaluate the overall health of our finances. Yet people with thriving Financial Wellbeing talk about a general sense of financial security (and lack of worry) instead of these absolute measures of wealth. So after reviewing the income levels of the people we interviewed, we conducted a deeper analysis of the key drivers of Financial Wellbeing.

What we found was that financial security — the perception that you have more than enough money to do what you want to do — has *three times the impact of your income alone* on overall wellbeing. Further, a lack of worry about money has more than double the impact of income on overall wellbeing.

Bookstore shelves are lined with advice about how to become rich, and most financial advisors are judged based on the monetary return they deliver. But this approach might be targeting the wrong outcome. Sure, it's important to save money for the future and maximize the return on your investments. But the outcome of wealth accumulation alone leads us astray.

Focusing solely on this goal can even reduce our wellbeing. There are plenty of people who make a lot of money but don't feel financially secure, and they worry about money regularly, which in turn drains their wellbeing. Conversely, there are lots of people with lower incomes who *do* feel financially secure and worry very little about money, which builds up their wellbeing.

Investing to Minimize Stress

People with thriving Financial Wellbeing are satisfied with their standard of living, don't worry about money in their everyday lives, and have confidence in their financial future. What we learned from this group is that financial security is both possible and practical for people across the range of income levels.

Robert is a minister who has high Financial Wellbeing. He described how he lived in a house that was "beyond his wildest imagination." And he had enough money to buy a nice recreational vehicle, which allowed his family to travel. "It's like there's no limit to what we can do," he said. "And I will tell you, 40 years ago when I was going into the ministry, if you had told me I was going to be living as good at this point, I'd have thought you were crazy."

Robert made all this possible by investing his money wisely. He routinely consulted with a financial advisor and his father, who is a tax attorney, about how to invest for the long term. As Robert and others with thriving Financial Wellbeing revealed, they are able to have a great deal of enjoyment with a moderate amount of money — and without the undue stress that can come with higher levels of risk and debt.

Many financial gurus would caution you not to pay off your home early — because of lower historical returns and tax deductibility. But several people we interviewed went against that conventional wisdom, not because it was the best way to accumulate great wealth, but because it gave them the daily satisfaction and comfort of not being in debt. And while some traditional experts would contend that it's important to keep a large amount of your portfolio in stock, some people with thriving Financial Wellbeing did not. They chose to ignore this advice (and the potential upside return) in favor of more conservative strategies that would not leave them worrying about where the stock market was headed each day.

When a wealth-accumulation strategy creates daily stress, it's not worth the potential return. If a major purchase such as a home or a car creates a burden of debt that makes you uncomfortable, it's likely to do more damage than good for your overall wellbeing. In short, managing your finances well allows you to do *what* you want to do *when* you want to do it.

The Essentials of Financial Wellbeing

People with thriving Financial Wellbeing are satisfied with their overall standard of living. They manage their personal finances well to create financial security. This eliminates day-to-day stress caused by debt and helps build financial reserves. People with high Financial Wellbeing spend their money wisely. They buy experiences that provide them with lasting memories.

They give to others and don't just spend on themselves. As a result of managing their money wisely, they have the financial freedom to spend even more time with the people whose company they enjoy most.

Three Recommendations for Boosting Financial Wellbeing:

1. Buy *experiences* — such as vacations and outings with friends or loved ones.

2. Spend on others instead of solely on material possessions.

3. Establish default systems (automated payments and savings) that lessen daily worry about money.

4: Physical Wellbeing

With every bite and drink we take, we make a choice: We can select something that is a *net positive* and benefits our health or we can choose something that is a *net negative*.

There are hundreds of moments every week when we make these seemingly small — but eventually significant — decisions. When we make a net positive choice (e.g., ordering salmon with a side of broccoli), it can improve our mood for the rest of the day — and in the long term, reduce our chances of getting diabetes, heart disease, and cancer. When we make a net negative choice (e.g., ordering a cheeseburger and fries), it can decrease our energy for the rest of the day — and over the years, raise our glucose and cholesterol levels.

New research suggests that a single meal high in saturated fat reduces our arteries' ability to carry enough blood to our bodies and brains. According to NYU's Gerald Weissmann, M.D., this "high-fat hangover" could also slow us down and impair our thinking: "A long weekend spent eating hot dogs, french fries, and pizza in Orlando might be great for our taste buds, but they might send our muscles and brains out to lunch."

If we choose a balance of good and bad foods, paired with a moderate amount of sleep and exercise, our body runs closer to average. But if we make substantially more net positive decisions about what we eat and drink, coupled with a good night's sleep and vigorous exercise, our bodies will run much more efficiently. Throughout the day, we make small choices whenever we decide whether or not to add creamer to our morning coffee, to snack on the pastries at our afternoon meeting, and to choose water or a sugary soda with dinner.

We make net negative decisions without thinking about the long-term consequences, even if we understand that they are harmful. Simply knowing that eating fried foods puts us at a 30% greater risk for a heart attack down the road doesn't change our short-term decisions. Much like the discovery of a connection between smoking and lung cancer several decades ago didn't cause millions of people to quit right away, a basic awareness of what foods are bad for us is not going to cure diabetes or obesity.

To make major lifestyle changes, we need to understand how a poor diet or a sedentary lifestyle affects us *today*. When we see the connection between short-term incentives enabling us to make net positive decisions in the moment, it helps us reach our longer term goals. The reality is that these net positive and net negative decisions accumulate over the years and shape our lives. So if we are able to make more net positive decisions throughout each day, it will create benefits that could last for generations.

Silencing Your Genes

When you visit the doctor, you're usually asked detailed questions about your family history of heart disease, cancer, and other conditions. Physicians ask these questions because they know that our genetic history is one way to predict our future health. Some genes boost our chances of being healthier and avoiding major health problems, while others predispose us to a wide range of conditions.

Given the influence that our genes have, it's easy to feel as if a lot of our health is beyond our control. After all, we can't just change our genes or re-sequence our DNA. However, new research is revealing that we might be able to control the *expression* of our genes. So even if you have a gene that predisposes you to a chronic disease, there are things you can do to either silence or amplify the expression of that gene.

One study found that men who have a specific gene that predisposes them to prostate cancer were able to suppress the expression of this gene substantially by eating the equivalent of just one portion of broccoli per week. To a certain degree, we *can* control the amplification or suppression of how our genes affect our health over a lifetime. And we might even be able to influence what is passed along to the next generation.

Protecting Your Genes for Future Generations

For years, scientists have thought that our genes were the only way biological traits were passed down through generations, but this conventional wisdom is turning out to be false. Instead, biologists are discovering that events during our lifetime can be passed on not only to our children, *but also to future generations*. This newly discovered phenomenon, known as "epigenetic inheritance," is much more common than we think.

For example, studies suggest that if you were malnourished during adolescence, your children *and your grandchildren* will be more susceptible to heart disease and diabetes. Experiments with animals show that epigenetic changes could be traced several generations downstream in certain species. So as an added incentive for improving your own health for the next few hours, weeks, and months, consider that your lifestyle choices might also influence the health of your children and grandchildren.

Food for Your Mood

The food we eat has a profound effect on our health, daily experiences, and how long we live. For example, a study of 60,000 women revealed that eating one or more servings of fatty fish (e.g., salmon) per week could reduce the risk of kidney cancer by 74%. This is likely due to the high content of omega-3 fatty acids in fatty fish. Higher levels of omega-3 fatty acids have been shown to be protective against a wide range of cancers, cognitive degeneration such as Alzheimer's, heart disease, and a wide range of other conditions. Other studies have revealed how high levels of omega-3s moderate symptoms of depression, decrease impulsiveness, and boost our daily mood.

Our early ancestors maintained a 2:1 ratio of omega-6s (found in meat and vegetable oils) to omega-3s (from fish, nuts, and seeds). In Western countries, that ratio has now spiked to as high as 10:1. A 2009 experiment that explored the consumption ratio of omega-6 fatty acids to omega-3s might explain why the consumption of omega-3s also decreases inflammation (pain), asthma, diabetes, and arthritis.

In this experiment, researchers fed healthy people a controlled diet that mimicked our early ancestors' diet (2:1) to see if it would create physiological changes. They discovered that many critical signaling genes that promote inflammation, autoimmune, and allergic responses were markedly reduced in *just five weeks* due to these dietary changes.

Scientists are learning a great deal about how dietary choices accumulate over a lifetime, and these choices also influence how hungry we are. While the conventional wisdom is that an empty stomach is the primary trigger of hunger, this might not be the case. Instead, the foods we eat might be tricking our body into thinking it needs more fat, thus starting a vicious cycle. When we eat meals high in carbohydrates and sugars, it essentially damages our appetite-control cells and sends a message to our brain to consume more, even if we don't need more food at that time. This could explain why portion size has spiraled out of control, particularly in cultures where typical diets include high levels of sugars and carbohydrates.

Healthier (unsaturated) fats such as those found in avocados, nuts, and olive oil send the *opposite* message and signal our brain to *stop* eating. We might tell ourselves that a handful of potato chips will tide us over for a bit, but that "harmless" snack could actually cause us to eat more — whereas a handful of nuts or vegetables would have the desired effect.

One caveat: not just any vegetable has health-protective effects. In the study that found that one portion of broccoli per week warded off prostate cancer, the researchers also followed a control group who ate a serving of peas (in place of the broccoli). In comparison to the broccoli group, the group that consumed one serving of peas per week for 12 months did not see significant changes in gene expression.

As you walk through a grocery store, one simple way to sort through what foods are best is to look for fruits and vegetables that have darker tones of red, green, and blue. Look for reds in apples, tomatoes, strawberries, raspberries, red peppers, radishes, chili peppers, and pomegranates. Healthy greens include broccoli, asparagus, artichokes, spinach, sprouts, lettuce, arugula, collard greens, kale, or Swiss chard. Blue tones include blueberries, blackberries, cabbage, and grapes.

It's also important to look out for the smaller net negatives we consume, often without even thinking about it: toppings, dressings, snacks, and drinks. These are often full of calories, sugars, and fats, and they can quickly turn a net positive main course into a net negative meal. The key is opting for healthier foods at each turn; they curb our hunger for a longer period of time while boosting our energy levels in the process.

20 Minutes of Exercise Boosts Our Mood for a Day

Even using conservative estimates, the majority of us do not get enough exercise. Just 38% of people we studied report that they have exercised or had a lot of physical activity in the past day. Among 400,000 Americans we surveyed in more depth, only 27% get the recommended 30 minutes or more of exercise five days per week.

People who exercise at least two days a week are happier and have significantly less stress. In addition, these benefits increase with more frequent exercise. We found that each additional day of exercise in a given week — at least up to six days when people reach a point of diminishing returns — continues to boost energy levels.

A recent experiment revealed that just 20 minutes of exercise could improve our mood for several hours *after* we finish working out. Researchers monitored participants who rode a bike at moderate intensity and another group who did not exercise. Those who exercised for just 20 minutes had a significant improvement in their mood after 2, 4, 8, and 12 hours when compared to those who did not exercise.

As a Mayo Clinic publication stated: "A lack of energy often results from inactivity, not age." On days when you don't have 20 or 30 minutes to exercise, a mere 11 minutes of lifting weights has been shown to increase metabolic rate, which helps you burn more fat throughout the day. *Any* exercise is better than an entire day with no vigorous activity.

"Too Tired"? That's the Best Time to Exercise

It might seem counterintuitive, but one of the best ways to combat fatigue is by exercising. We might use being too tired as an excuse to avoid working out, but that's the worst time to skip exercise. A comprehensive analysis of more than 70 trials found that *exercising is much more effective at eliminating fatigue than prescription drugs* used for this purpose. This study also found that nearly everyone, from healthy adults to cancer patients and those with chronic disease conditions such as diabetes and heart disease, benefits from exercise.

One of the primary reasons people exercise regularly is because it makes them feel better about themselves and their appearance, and it boosts their confidence. If you exercise today, you are more than twice as likely to feel physically attractive *tomorrow*. Feeling attractive is not just important for our self-confidence. Researchers at Columbia University found that our psychological perceptions of our body image could be as important as objective measures like body mass index (BMI).

There is no age limit to having good exercise habits or thriving Physical Wellbeing. Dave, who is 88, responded with an exuberant "no" when we asked him if he had any health problems that prevent him from doing things other people his age can normally do. Dave reports that he has no daily pain. Perhaps it's because he gets up at 6:00 every morning, takes a long walk, does his own yard work and home repairs, and regularly fixes things for his children. As Dave put it, "I keep busy. And I read. I have a computer. I use it, because if you don't use all of your organs in your body, including your brain, you won't feel good."

While Dave is retired and doesn't travel as much as he used to, he still goes to annual golf outings with his friends and plays several rounds a year. Each day, he does 30 minutes of vigorous exercise in addition to his walks. He then adds at least 10 to 12 minutes a day doing stretching exercises. Even at 88, Dave feels great physically and has a good deal of confidence in his appearance. When we asked Dave what his doctor would say about the way he manages his health, he told us that he had just visited the doctor the day before, who enthusiastically said, "Whatever you're doing, just keep doing it!"

Sleep: Your Daily Reset Button

Along with healthy eating and regular exercise, sleep plays an essential role in our Physical Wellbeing. To study the value of quality sleep, we conducted an experiment that tracked the effect of a full night of sleep (or lack thereof) on the following day. People who felt irritable before going to sleep and then had a good night's sleep had above-average moods the next morning and afternoon. In contrast, for those who were in a good mood at the end of the day but did not get the right amount of sleep, their mood levels dropped to average, and they were more likely to feel irritable the next day.

Getting a good night's sleep is like hitting a reset button. It clears our stressors from the day before. Even if we have a bad day, getting a sound night of sleep gives us a fresh start on the next day. It also increases our chances of having energy and high wellbeing throughout the day.

But we're getting less sleep with each passing year, and we now sleep an average of 6.7 hours during a weeknight. This means that many of us are falling well short of the recommended seven to eight hours of sleep per night. As a result, we move slower, have trouble concentrating, become forgetful, make bad decisions, are more irritable, and show visible signs of sleeplessness.

Learning While You Sleep

Sleep serves a larger purpose than simply keeping us well-rested. Our brains are extraordinarily active when we are asleep. In fact, our learning may actually *accelerate* while we are sleeping. Scientists are discovering that we learn and make connections *more effectively when we are asleep* than we do when we are awake. Each night of sleep allows our brain to process what we learned the day before. As a result, we are more likely to remember what we learned if we get a sound night's sleep.

A 2004 study illustrates the importance of sleep and how it helps our brain mentally catalog what we have learned each day. A team of German researchers taught people how to solve a particular type of math problem using a complicated procedure. They asked the participants to practice the problem about 100 times. The participants were sent away and told to return 12 hours later. Then they were instructed to try it another 200 times.

What the researchers did not tell participants was that there was a much simpler way to solve the problem. Many of the people in the study discovered the shortcut over time. The critical differentiator — in terms of those who figured it out — was sleep. *Participants who slept between sessions were 2½ times more likely to figure it out* compared to those who stayed awake between sessions. The study revealed how the sleeping brain was actually solving a problem — even though the person did not know there was a problem to solve.

Sleep helps us synthesize the learning and experiences of a day. While we sleep, our brain is playing connect-the-dots until we wake up. And it likely does so more effectively than we could if we tried when we were awake. So while we have known all along that a good night's sleep helps the *next* day, it is just as important for encoding information we learned the day *before*.

The *Right* Amount of Sleep

Getting the right amount of sleep every night can be difficult. The majority of research suggests that — from a health, memory, appearance, and wellbeing standpoint — we need somewhere between seven and eight hours of sleep each night to get optimal benefits. Researchers have found that both short amounts (5-6 hours) and long durations (9-10 hours) of sleep can cause problems.

One study found that short-duration sleepers *and* long-duration sleepers have more health problems. Short-duration sleepers were 35% more likely to experience a substantial weight gain, and long-duration sleepers were 25% more likely to have a substantial weight gain. This might be due to a hormonal imbalance — caused by a sleepless night — that actually increases our appetite the next day. Over time, a lack of sleep has also been shown to increase the risk of type 2 diabetes and overall risk of death.

Fewer than seven hours of sleep also takes a toll on our immune system. A 2009 study found that *people who get less than seven hours of sleep were nearly three times as likely to develop a cold* when compared to those who get at least eight hours of sleep. So adding even 30 minutes or an hour of sleep could help us stay healthy, including warding off the common cold.

Positive Defaults for Your Health

Making the right choices *in advance* can help us get ahead of our short-term desires. For example, if we're able to make healthy choices in the supermarket, it is easier to control impulse eating when we open the refrigerator each evening. Even when making minor decisions such as where to go for lunch, the restaurant we choose might be more important than the decision we make when we order at the restaurant.

Fewer than 1 in 10 people even *claim* to be good at resisting the temptation of unhealthy options on a menu.

If we decide to go to a typical fast-food restaurant, we could be doomed from the start. Even if the restaurant has a couple healthy alternatives on the menu, the mere presence of these choices could be detrimental to our health. One experiment revealed that just having a healthy option on a menu (a side salad) actually made people *three times as likely to select an unhealthy option* (a side of french fries) when compared to a menu *without* the side salad as an option. So when the burger joint adds a healthy salad to its menu, it gives us an excuse to go there for lunch. Yet when we arrive — even if we told ourselves we were going there for a salad — most of us succumb to temptation and order the burger and fries.

But if we choose to have lunch at a restaurant that serves mostly healthy choices instead, it increases our odds of making a good decision at the last minute. Or if we prepare a nutritious lunch in advance and take it to work, that circumvents both of these opportunities for our short-term self to take over. The further we can get ahead of our immediate impulses by doing things like loading up on healthy foods at the grocery store, the more we boost our odds of making a healthy decision in the moment.

The Economics of Health

One aspect of our Physical Wellbeing that does not get enough attention is the physical and economic costs of being unhealthy. They are unmistakable and have frightening implications, both for individuals and for societies.

Roughly one-quarter of the world's population has a lot of physical pain on a daily basis and health problems that keep them from doing things other people their age normally can do. This equates to about *1.5 billion people who are not doing what they want to do today because of physical pain.* Even in a developed country like the United States, the percentages are alarmingly similar to this global average.

In addition to the sheer physical suffering, the economic costs are staggering. For example, in the United States, healthcare costs represent 16% of the total economy and are projected to reach 20% of the nation's Gross Domestic Product (GDP) in the next decade. In 1999, the cost of insuring a family in the United States was approximately $5,700. As of 2009, that cost has soared to more than $13,000, and according to projections, it will reach nearly $25,000 by 2018.

For too many Americans, poor health is not just a physical problem, but also a financial burden. Two out of three U.S. residents report having problems with medical bills, going without needed care, being underinsured, or living completely uninsured as a result of these soaring costs. According to a Harvard study, in 2007, 62% of all personal bankruptcies in the United States had a medical cause.

Under the current healthcare system in the United States, most people receive health benefits through their employer. These costs are shared and spread out across larger groups. So in most cases, Americans are paying not only for the cost of their own healthcare, but also for the collective medical expenses of their colleagues. As a result of how this system works, estimates show that each healthy American is paying a tax of an additional $1,464 per year because of colleagues who lead less healthy lifestyles. Other studies have found that *more than half* of all healthcare spending in the United States is consumed by just 5% of the population.

Further, 75% of medical costs are due to largely preventable conditions (stress, tobacco use, physical inactivity, and poor food choices). And, the United States' obesity rate is one of the highest in the world (33% — for comparison, some countries have 3%-4% obesity). If people in the United States could reverse the obesity epidemic in the same way that smoking was pushed to the edges of social networks, the societal *and* economic implications would be substantial. Clearly, Americans could save a great deal of money by leading healthier lifestyles.

What might be most encouraging, regardless of what country you live in, is the speed at which healthy lifestyle changes can improve even the most chronic conditions. Researchers studying type 2 diabetes, for example, found that by putting people on a healthier diet, they could significantly reduce glucose, triglycerides, and cholesterol, while decreasing the use of prescription medications by 43% — in just 4½ months. And as we mentioned earlier, a diet with the right balance of healthy foods was shown to alter the expression of genes that cause inflammation and allergies in just five weeks. This illustrates how the benefits of lifestyle changes can often be seen in days, weeks, and months.

The Essentials of Physical Wellbeing

People with thriving Physical Wellbeing effectively manage their health. They exercise regularly and feel better throughout the day as a result. They make good dietary choices, which keeps their energy high throughout the day and sharpens their thinking. They get enough sleep to wake up feeling well-rested and to process what they learned the day before — and to get a good start on the next day. People with thriving Physical Wellbeing look better, feel better, and will live longer.

Three Recommendations for Boosting Physical Wellbeing:

1. Get at least 20 minutes of physical activity each day — ideally in the morning to improve your mood throughout the day.

2. Sleep enough to feel well-rested (generally seven to eight hours) but not too long (more than nine hours).

3. Set positive defaults when you shop for groceries. Load up on natural foods that are red, green, and blue.

5: Community Wellbeing

Community Wellbeing isn't the first thing people think about when they evaluate their overall wellbeing. But this element can actually be *the differentiator between a good life and a great one.*

Community Wellbeing starts with some of the basics. While you might not think about the quality of the water you drink or the air you breathe every day, a lack of security about these fundamental needs can cause significant concern over time. Feeling safe walking alone at night in your neighborhood and having confidence that you won't be harmed or assaulted is another primary necessity.

In countries around the world — particularly in developing nations — millions of people report that they do not have this security. Even in the United States, United Kingdom, France, Germany, and parts of Western Europe and Australia, as many as one in three people don't feel safe walking alone at night where they live. In the United States, residents of several cities have serious concerns about safety, air pollution, and other environmental contaminants. When these needs aren't met, it is difficult to have thriving wellbeing.

The Perfect Place for You

Once you have a basic sense of security, the next level of Community Wellbeing is living in an area that is a good fit for your personality, family, interests, and other pursuits. John, who has thriving Community Wellbeing, described his city this way: "It's a little slower paced than your average city. Very outdoorsy. If you like outdoor activities, this is a good place. Clean, good schools, and you can feel safe walking around in any part of the city any time of day or night, and the cost of living is a lot cheaper here than where we were previously."

While the things that make a community "perfect" will be different for everyone, people use common themes to describe ideal communities. One of the most important factors is aesthetics, which includes naturally beautiful places and the availability of parks, trails, and playgrounds. Another key differentiator is social offerings, or places where people can meet, spend time with friends, and enjoy the nightlife. The third quality that distinguishes near-perfect communities from the rest is a general openness to all types of people, regardless of race, heritage, age, or sexual orientation.

However, just living in the right place is unlikely to create thriving Community Wellbeing. This requires active involvement in community groups or organizations. Many people belong to groups that connect them to a wider network of friends or acquaintances. Participating in outreach programs to clean up the community, feed those in need, or help children learn fosters their Community Wellbeing. Rosa, who has thriving Community Wellbeing, described how her church makes a conscious effort to focus on the wellbeing of the community's residents. Her involvement helps her make a connection with a broader group.

Unless you make an effort to get involved in social groups, it is unlikely that your Community Wellbeing will grow. Many people claim to live in strong communities, but they acknowledge that they like to keep to themselves — and as a result, most of these people have lower Community Wellbeing. Even for those who are not naturally sociable, just signing up, opting into an event, or initiating some contact with community groups can boost overall wellbeing. Thriving Community Wellbeing is about what we do to *give back* to our community.

Well-*Doing*: The Pinnacle of a Life Well-Lived?

"Give blood. All you'll feel is good."

As this slogan from an American Red Cross campaign illustrates, giving is good for *both* the recipient and the donor. Psychologists have conducted experiments to determine if this Red Cross claim is true — and it turns out that this is one slogan that passes the truth-in-advertising test. People reported experiencing increased moods *before* and *after* they donated blood.

At the highest end of the Community Wellbeing continuum is giving back to society. This may be what differentiates an exceptional life from a good one. When we asked people with thriving wellbeing about the greatest contribution they had made in their life, with few exceptions, they mentioned the impact they have had on another person, group, or community. Not only had these individuals made a substantial contribution to something bigger than themselves, but they also had been recognized for their community involvement.

As we mentioned in the section on Financial Wellbeing, donating money results in a greater return for our wellbeing than buying material goods for ourselves. Neuroscientists have discovered that the regions of the brain that are activated when we receive money (based on fMRI brain scans) glow even brighter when we *give* money. According to Jordan Grafman, a neuroscientist at the National Institutes of Health, these reactions in the brain "help us plan into the future, feel emotionally closer to others, and give us a sense of reward after a behavior — which reinforces that behavior, making it more likely we will do the same thing again."

We often get a sense of joy from giving a meaningful gift to a loved one, but perhaps no gift is as valuable as *our time*. This might explain why some volunteers get a "helper's high" — they feel stronger, more energetic, and more motivated after helping others even in the smallest ways. When we surveyed more than 23,000 people on this topic, nearly 9 in 10 reported "getting an emotional boost" from doing kind things for other people.

When we do things for others, we see how we can make a difference, and this gives us confidence in our own ability to create change. Throughout the course of our lives, well-doing promotes deeper social interaction, enhanced meaning and purpose, and a more active lifestyle — while keeping us from being too preoccupied with ourselves or getting into harmful emotional states. Several studies have shown a link between altruistic behavior and increases in overall longevity, and researchers have speculated that this might be due in part to how *well-doing inoculates us against stress and negative emotions.*

Opting Into Involvement

When presented with two choices, we tend to select the default option. Even in the case of something as significant as donating your organs, your decision is heavily influenced by whether the system is set up to opt you in or to opt you out. The basic structure of a form, a pre-filled check box, or an automatic enrollment process shapes our decisions a lot more than we realize.

For example, in countries where citizens are automatically enrolled to donate their organs as the default, the vast majority choose to do so. However, when citizens are not automatically enrolled, very few choose to donate their organs.

Opt In vs. Opt Out

Where the default is set and its influence on our decisions

Rate of Organ Donation by Country

Individual Must Opt In		
NETHERLANDS	27.5%	👤👤👤👤👤👤👤
UNITED KINGDOM	17.2%	👤👤👤👤
GERMANY	12.0%	👤👤👤
DENMARK	4.3%	👤

Individual Must Opt Out		
AUSTRIA	99.9%	👤👤👤👤👤👤👤👤👤👤👤👤👤👤👤👤👤👤👤👤👤👤👤👤👤
FRANCE	99.9%	👤👤👤👤👤👤👤👤👤👤👤👤👤👤👤👤👤👤👤👤👤👤👤👤👤
HUNGARY	99.9%	👤👤👤👤👤👤👤👤👤👤👤👤👤👤👤👤👤👤👤👤👤👤👤👤👤
PORTUGAL	99.6%	👤👤👤👤👤👤👤👤👤👤👤👤👤👤👤👤👤👤👤👤👤👤👤👤👤
POLAND	99.5%	👤👤👤👤👤👤👤👤👤👤👤👤👤👤👤👤👤👤👤👤👤👤👤👤👤
BELGIUM	98.0%	👤👤👤👤👤👤👤👤👤👤👤👤👤👤👤👤👤👤👤👤👤👤👤👤
SWEDEN	89.5%	👤👤👤👤👤👤👤👤👤👤👤👤👤👤👤👤👤👤👤👤👤👤

Adapted from Johnson and Goldstein, *Science*, 2003

Where this default option is set might even determine whether millions live or die each year. In China, for example, more than 1 million people are reported to be in need of organ donations, yet only 1% actually receive the transplant surgery they need. Because of the nation's organ shortage, four in five people die while waiting for a transplant. The rate of organ donation in China is a mere *one-third of one percent*. But if every Chinese citizen were opted in to organ donation, the supply could exceed the need.

For the most part, we can set our own defaults — for everything from organ donation to savings plans. But it does require some effort. So we often sit back and let life happen over the course of years and decades. But people with thriving Community Wellbeing find novel ways to opt in to regular donations and volunteering.

One man we interviewed told us he volunteers at organizations that he knows will make specific requests of his time every month, much like a part-time job. One woman holds herself accountable for at least five hours of volunteering per month. Several people described how they give a fixed amount each year or a fixed percentage of their income to community groups.

Some organizational leaders make it easy for employees to have regular contributions deducted directly from their paycheck. Progressive workplaces offer matching company funds for each dollar contributed by their employees. While the ways in which individuals and organizations do so vary, they all establish some kind of mechanism to hold themselves accountable for sustained community involvement.

It's OK to Make It Personal

Giving back to the community does not have to be a purely altruistic act. People who make profound contributions to community organizations usually have an emotional tie to the organization's mission or cause. People get involved because of a parent with a degenerative disease, a friend with cancer, a child with autism, or some other deeply personal connection — it is these connections that spark their interest in the first place. Those with a vested interest actually have *more to offer* because of all their knowledge and personal mission.

People with high Community Wellbeing make their interests known to friends, colleagues, and family members. Then when the right opportunity presents itself, they are more likely to be called upon, and they get involved. Because this often occurs in the context of a workplace or a religious organization, these are good forums for telling others about your interests.

Increasing Wellbeing Throughout Your Community

As we mentioned earlier, major societal changes like the decline in smoking rates occur in the context of social networks. Most people did not quit smoking on their own. They quit because it was no longer socially acceptable to smoke. Their friends quit, local restaurants banned them from smoking, and their employers literally left them standing outside in the cold. As smokers were pushed to the outer edges of their communities, they finally kicked the habit.

This is just one example of how groups, communities, and organizations can create positive social change. Alcoholics Anonymous leverages relationships and fosters positive group pressure to help people stay sober. Weight Watchers brings people together to lose weight. These efforts are successful, in large part, because they draw on positive peer pressure, social support, and accountability to others.

Experimental research suggests that creating sustainable change may be two to three times as likely to happen in the context of a group, company, or community organization. For example, if you enroll in an intensive weight-loss program *alone*, *hmm . . .*

there is a 24% chance that you will maintain your weight loss after 10 months. If you enroll in the same program and then join a social support group of three strangers, there is a nearly 50% chance you will maintain the weight loss 10 months later. But if you enroll in the program *with three friends or colleagues you already know*, the odds of maintaining your weight loss go up to 66%.

As part of Gallup's global research, we routinely ask people if they have volunteered in the past month. Across 150 countries, we found that people who are engaged in their *careers* are 20%-30% more likely to give back to their *community*. In one organization we studied, workers who were the most engaged in their jobs donated 2.6 times more than those who were not engaged in their careers. Community Wellbeing is interconnected with, and builds directly on, the other four elements. So as your wellbeing improves in other areas, your odds of having thriving Community Wellbeing dramatically increase as well.

The Essentials of Community Wellbeing

People with high Community Wellbeing feel safe and secure where they live. They take pride in their community, and they believe it is headed in the right direction. This often results in their wanting to give back and make a lasting contribution to society. People with thriving Community Wellbeing have identified areas where they can contribute to their community based on their own strengths and passions. They tell others about these interests to connect with the right groups and causes. Their contribution may start small, but over time, it leads to more involvement and has a profound impact on their community. The efforts of people with thriving Community Wellbeing are what create communities we cannot imagine living without.

Three Recommendations for Boosting Community Wellbeing:

1. Identify how you can contribute to your community based on your personal mission.

2. Tell people about your passions and interests so they can connect you with relevant groups and causes.

3. Opt in to a community group or event. Even if you start small, start now.

Concluding Thoughts: Measuring What Makes Life Worthwhile

As Bobby Kennedy said just a few months before his death in 1968, we continue to gauge the progress of our lives, our organizations, and our communities based on narrow and shallow measures:

We seem to have surrendered community excellence and community values in the mere accumulation of material things. Our gross domestic product . . . if we should judge America by that — counts air pollution and cigarette advertising, and ambulances to clear our highways of carnage. It counts special locks for our doors and jails for the people who break them. It counts the destruction of our redwoods and the loss of our natural wonder in chaotic sprawl. It counts napalm and the cost of a nuclear warhead, and armored cars for police who fight riots in our streets. It counts Whitman's rifle and Speck's knife, and the television programs which glorify violence in order to sell toys to our children.

Yet the gross domestic product does not allow for the health of our children, the quality of their education, or the joy of their play. It does not include the beauty of our poetry or the strength of our marriages; the intelligence of our public debate or the integrity of our public officials. It measures neither wit nor courage; neither our wisdom nor our learning; neither our compassion nor our devotion to our country; it measures everything, in short, except that which makes life worthwhile.

As Kennedy so eloquently described, our lives are the composite of much more than our economic output. To create a life that's worthwhile, not just for ourselves but for those around us, we need to find something we love to do that benefits society. We need to invest time strengthening our relationships with the people we love. We need enough financial security to provide for our families' needs. We need to adopt lifestyles that give us the health and energy to keep moving each day.

We also need to make better choices *in the moment*. As Nobel Prize-winning economist Thomas Schelling described, we behave as if we're two different people: one who wants a lean body and another who wants dessert.

Even small short-term differences in how we allocate our time can result in better days. An extra half-hour of sleep or an extra hour of social time can be the difference between a great day and a mediocre day. Changing our daily routine a little can have a big impact on the quality of each day.

On a given day, we might sit around and respond to problems at work instead of initiating. We might passively watch TV rather than getting out and exercising. Or maybe we spend on something now that creates stress in a few weeks or months. We might even think about doing something to give back to our community, but decide we'll do it later and never get around to it. Days like this start a vicious cycle.

Just one day when we eat poorly, skip exercising, are stressed at work, don't get enough social time, and worry about money leads to a host of negative outcomes. On days like this, we have less energy, we look worse, we don't treat people well, and we get a lousy night's sleep. As a result, we miss the reset provided by a sound night of sleep, and the cycle continues.

When we break this downward spiral and get a good night's sleep, we're off to the right start. This allows us to wake up refreshed and increases our chances of exercising in the morning. If we can use our strengths at our job every day, this connects our daily activities to a much higher purpose and allows us to get more done. Between work and time with our friends and family, if we can get in six hours of social time, chances are, we'll have 10 times as many good moments as stressful ones.

One of the best ways to create more good days is by setting positive defaults. Any time you help your short-term self work *with* your long-term self, you have an opportunity. You can intentionally choose to spend more time with the people you enjoy most and engage your strengths as much as possible. You can structure your finances to minimize the worry caused by debt. You can make exercise a standard part of your routine. You can make healthier decisions in the supermarket so you don't have to trust yourself when you have a craving a few days later. And you can make commitments to community, religious, or volunteer groups, knowing that you will follow through once you've signed up in advance. Through these daily choices, you create stronger friendships, families, workplaces, and communities.

Additional Tools
and Resources

A: The Wellbeing Finder: Measuring and Managing Your Wellbeing

Management requires measurement. If you want to improve your wellbeing and the wellbeing of those around you, you first need to know where you stand. Once you have a baseline measure, it is easier to improve your wellbeing in each of the five elements.

So to help you get started, we have included a unique access code in the packet at the end of this book that is valid for a complimentary subscription to Gallup's Wellbeing program. This code will allow you to access the Wellbeing website and take the Wellbeing Finder, an assessment that measures your progress in each of the five essential elements of wellbeing over time.

When you take the Wellbeing Finder, you will receive a scorecard with your overall wellbeing score as well as your score in each of the five areas: Career Wellbeing, Social Wellbeing, Financial Wellbeing, Physical Wellbeing, and Community Wellbeing. Based on your responses to the Wellbeing Finder, scores are categorized into three zones:

- **Thriving:** Your wellbeing is strong, consistent, and progressing. (Overall wellbeing score of 70-100)

- **Struggling:** Your wellbeing is moderate or inconsistent. (Overall wellbeing score of 40-69)

- **Suffering:** Your wellbeing is at high risk. (Overall wellbeing score of 0-39)

Each time you take the Wellbeing Finder, the website will store your results so you can trend your wellbeing over time, identifying areas that need more attention as well as areas of strength that you can continue to build on. You can also compare your scores with others' scores based on age, gender, income, and education levels.

Our research suggests that as your overall wellbeing score increases, you will see substantive changes in your daily life. Even incremental gains in your overall Wellbeing Finder score can lead to more days when you feel healthier, have more energy, and can achieve more. Even if you already have high levels of wellbeing, small gains in overall wellbeing can lead to much better days. For example, people with a total Wellbeing Finder score in the 70s have *three times* as many unhealthy days in a month compared with those who have a total score in the 90s.

High Wellbeing = Fewer Sick Days

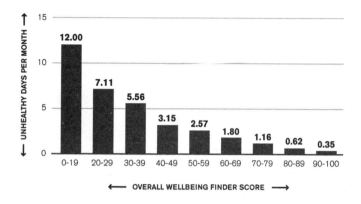

When we selected the questions for the Wellbeing Finder, we went to great lengths to ensure that the core elements the assessment measures are *within your control* (e.g., exercising regularly). This is an important distinction, as countless studies have shown that our genes predetermine a portion of our total wellbeing. Essentially, much like our weight, some people start at a higher baseline level of wellbeing. Yet most of the overall variability is within our control based on what we do throughout the course of our lifetime.

And much like you can make choices to control your weight, you can take actionable steps to boost your scores within each of the five elements of wellbeing. As part of the Wellbeing program, you can create customized action plans for improving your wellbeing. To help you focus on achievable goals, you can choose from suggested action items based on your results to the Wellbeing Finder, or you can create your own.

Simply put, it is quite possible to improve a great deal in *all* of these areas over time, regardless of your starting point. So a low score in one area of wellbeing certainly doesn't mean that you are in a hopeless situation. Instead, a score below the thriving zone just indicates that you have substantial room for improvement and growth. When you move into the thriving zone in any of the five areas of wellbeing, you are likely to see improvements in your daily wellbeing and in the way you evaluate your life overall.

Some people have a natural predisposition toward higher Career Wellbeing, while others will have a head start in terms of their Social Wellbeing or Physical Wellbeing. But the most meaningful comparison is not how you measure up to others. What's *most important* is how your scores compare with your *own* personal baseline. Taking the Wellbeing Finder once provides some initial insight. But the real test is whether your scores, overall and in each domain, increase or decrease over time. The Wellbeing Finder and accompanying program allow you to chart your progress over the span of weeks, months, years, and decades.

Your Wellbeing by Domain

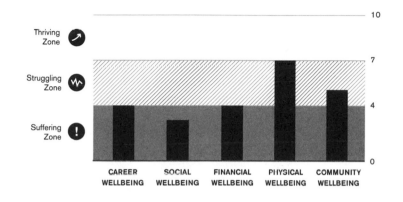

Your Overall Wellbeing

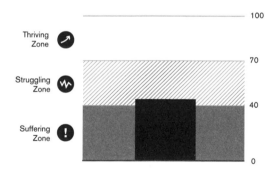

Tracking Your Daily Experiences

In addition to this broad evaluation of your life, access to the Wellbeing website will allow you to take the Daily Tracker, a brief assessment about your daily experiences. This survey shows you how things are going for you *right now*.

In contrast to the Wellbeing Finder, which is designed to be taken less frequently (monthly or quarterly), you can use this shorter subset of questions daily or weekly to measure your wellbeing trend at a more detailed level. Because this is an immediate gauge of how you are doing, taking the Daily Tracker will help you see what influences your daily experiences.

We developed the questions in the Daily Tracker survey to summarize whether people in different parts of the world were having good days (ones they would like to have more of) or bad days (days they would like to forget about). To capture the entirety of a given day, these questions ask you to reflect on yesterday in particular. Some of the questions are about positive experiences (feeling well-rested, being treated with respect, smiling or laughing, learning or doing something interesting, and enjoyment). Others are about negative experiences or feelings (physical pain, worry, sadness, stress, and anger). While there are several elements that factor into how you evaluate your day, these were the most effective questions across a broad range of countries and life situations.

Your Daily Tracker score ranges from 0-10, and — like your Wellbeing Finder score — you can compare your Daily Tracker score with various demographic groups on the Wellbeing website. And in Appendix F and Appendix G in this book, you can review the Daily Experience scores for residents of U.S. states, cities, countries, and regions throughout the world.

On the Wellbeing website, you can record specific events that occur during the day so that you can see how these moments influence your wellbeing. Your Daily Tracker results help you identify the people, places, and things that contribute to the days when your wellbeing is thriving — or when it is struggling or suffering — so you can quickly recognize the patterns in your life that affect your daily experiences. Measuring your wellbeing on a regular basis and changing your behaviors based on these patterns should lead to sustained improvement in your overall wellbeing.

Which of the Five Elements Is Most Important?

You might wonder which of the five essential elements of wellbeing — Career, Social, Financial, Physical, or Community — is the most important. We arranged the five element chapters in the beginning of this book based on their order of importance — for the *average* person we surveyed. This means that, on average, Career Wellbeing has slightly more influence than Physical Wellbeing or Community Wellbeing. Yet every one of the five elements is a robust predictor of various life outcomes. And, for instance, some of us would prioritize our Physical Wellbeing ahead of our Financial Wellbeing. For this reason, we give equal weight to each of these five areas in the Wellbeing program, so you can decide what's most important based on your own situation.

B: Daily Wellbeing: How We Spend Our Time

While the five essential elements of wellbeing represent a comprehensive *evaluation* of our lives as a whole, our daily *experience* is another important piece of the puzzle. Momentary experiences accumulate and shape our lives. And it's within these daily experiences that we begin to create real behavioral change. To understand how specific experiences affect our wellbeing, leading psychologists and economists have spent a great deal of time over the past decade exploring this topic.

Recently, a team that included three of Gallup's senior scientists (a Nobel prize-winning psychologist, the current Chief Economist of the U.S. Department of Treasury, and a leader in the field of real-time data capture) proposed a formal approach dubbed National Time Accounting for measuring how we use our time. This research provides a unique lens into our daily experiences. It also reveals the specific activities we enjoy most and the groups of people we most (and least) enjoy spending time with.

As part of this time-use research, participants (interviewed by Gallup) were asked how much time they spent involved in 45 different activities — ranging from the infrequent, such as attending a sporting event, to the more frequent, such as watching television and working. Because many of the 45 activities represented less than 1% of the total time we spend in a day, the researchers grouped them into six general categories.

How We Spend Our Time
By general category

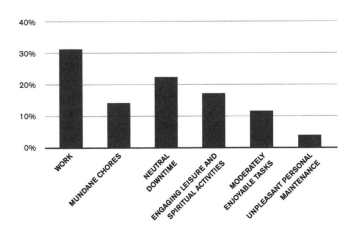

Adapted from Krueger, et al., *National Time Accounting: The Currency of Life*, March 2008

The *Activities* We Enjoy Most

To calculate how much we enjoy doing certain activities, the researchers created a formula that accounted for each person's self-reported levels of happiness, tiredness, stress, sadness, interest, and pain while participating in each activity. This allowed the researchers to compare how time spent in each of these areas influenced daily wellbeing. As you can see from the following chart, people report having the highest levels of happiness and interest (paired with lower levels of tiredness, stress, sadness, and pain) when they are engaged in leisure and spiritual activities.

Overall Enjoyment by Category

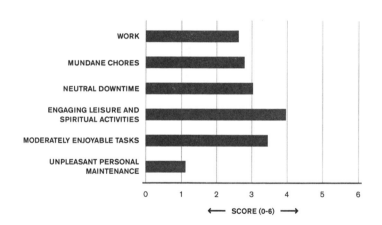

Adapted from Krueger, et al., *National Time Accounting: The Currency of Life,* March 2008

While these six general categories describe the overall distribution of our time, when it comes to how we spend our time on a daily basis, the 45 specific activities are even more revealing. As you can see in the following chart, there is a considerable range in the levels of enjoyment we get from different activities.

10 Most Enjoyable Activities

ACTIVITIES	SCORE
Listening to music	4.81
Playing with children	4.81
Attending sporting event	4.74
Hunting, fishing, boating, hiking	4.73
Parties or receptions	4.72
Purchase personal services	4.43
General out-of-home leisure	4.39
Cafe or bar	4.39
Sports and exercise	4.26
Worship and religious acts	4.24

10 Least Enjoyable Activities

ACTIVITIES	SCORE
Personal medical care	0.21
Financial/government services	0.32
Homework	0.80
Purchase medical services	2.08
Home/vehicle maintenance	2.22
Set table, wash/put away dishes	2.28
Paid work in home	2.35
Schooling/education	2.42
Laundry/ironing/clothing repair	2.46
Main paid work (not at home)	2.55

Adapted from Krueger, et al., *National Time Accounting: The Currency of Life*, March 2008

Listening to music, for example, is one of the most enjoyable activities not only because people report being happier when they're listening to music, but also because it is associated with extremely low levels of stress. Playing with children (which is tied for the most enjoyable activity) actually increases happiness more than listening to music does. But playing with children is also associated with slightly higher stress levels compared with listening to music.

When reviewing this comprehensive list of activities in conjunction with trends (based on surveys conducted in the 1960s, 1970s, 1980s, 1990s, and within the last decade), one pattern that emerges is a dramatic increase in the amount of time men *and* women spend watching television. In the 1960s, women spent about 8% of their time in a given day watching television. Today, women spend nearly 15% of their time watching television or videos. Men spent about 11% of their time watching television in the 1960s. Today, that number has increased to more than 17% of their total time in a day.

It's worth noting that time spent watching television falls somewhere in the middle (mean score of 2.94) when it comes to enjoyment. People do not report that the time they spend watching television is anywhere near as enjoyable compared with time out with friends or time spent playing with children. In the United States in particular, the substantial amount of time spent watching television might not be doing much direct harm, but people would likely have more happiness and interest in their lives if they spent more of their time in active, social pursuits.

That being said, Gallup's global research suggests that television could be a net positive in most households around the world. Our international studies reveal that people who have televisions in their homes, on average, report having higher wellbeing than those who do not have televisions at home. These differences are substantial; people who have TVs in their homes have about 10% higher overall wellbeing and are more optimistic about the future.

Regardless of things like wealth, access to electricity, and running water, the benefits of TV ownership endure. Even when comparing people with identical incomes, TV owners around the world still enjoy higher levels of wellbeing and optimism. These results suggest that, on a global scale, owning a television might have a real benefit. In developing countries, for example, it is likely that television provides access to basic information, learning, and a connection to what is going on in other parts of the world.

Who We Enjoy Being Around

Across all of our studies on daily wellbeing, we found that one of the best predictors of good days versus bad days is the *amount of time* people spend around friends and family members. The aforementioned team of scientists created an "Unpleasant index" (U-index) to measure the percentage of time people spend in an unpleasant state when they are with a specific person. This index is the proportion of time that ratings of negative feelings ("depressed," "angry," "frustrated") exceed ratings of positive feelings ("happy," "enjoy myself," "friendly").

The People We *Don't* Like to Be Around

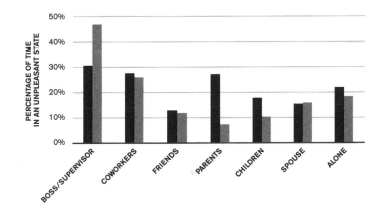

Adapted from Krueger, et al., *National Time Accounting: The Currency of Life,* March 2008

As you can see in the previous graph, spending time with the boss is *two to four times as unpleasant* as spending time with friends. This is even more pronounced for men, who report unusually high levels of stress and low levels of happiness when they spend time with their manager or supervisor.

Even though time spent with your boss is, on average, the worst time of the day, it doesn't have to be. Our studies show that there are thousands of managers who have reversed this pattern and have improved the engagement and lives of their employees as they improve their organization's performance.

Considering the effect of Career Wellbeing on our physiology, these findings highlight the need for managers, leaders, and organizations to think more consciously about the impact they have on each employee's wellbeing. And given how much time we spend at work, there may well be more opportunity to increase our daily wellbeing in this area than in any other domain.

C: Increasing Wellbeing in Organizations: The Role of Managers and Leaders

---

If you lead or manage people, your actions have a direct impact on the wellbeing of others. When leaders embrace the opportunity to improve employees' wellbeing, they create more engaging places to work and greater returns for the organization. And they even help strengthen their employees' families. But when leaders opt to ignore employees' wellbeing — dismissing it as something that's "none of their business" — they erode the confidence of those who follow them and limit their organization's ability to grow.

Over the past decade, Gallup has worked with hundreds of organizations to help their managers create engagement and boost the wellbeing of their employees. One of the best questions we have asked more than 15 million workers is whether their supervisor (or someone at work) seems to care about them as a person. Implicit in this question is the notion that an employee's manager or supervisor cares about him as a whole person, not merely as an employee or as a means to an end. This question serves as a barometer of whether an employee feels as if his manager truly cares about his wellbeing.

What we've discovered is that the world's best managers see the growth of each employee as an end in itself, instead of as a means to an end. They realize that each worker's wellbeing, and in many cases the wellbeing of his or her entire family, is largely dependent on their ability to lead and manage. Ritz-Carlton President Simon Cooper told us how he sees the greater purpose of his organization as serving not only its 38,000 employees around the world, but also their families. This type of progressive thinking is not uncommon among the best leaders we interviewed, as they often consider the broader influence they have on their followers and the networks that surround them.

Mervyn Davies, the former chairman of Standard Chartered Bank, described how he helped more than 70,000 bank employees (across 70 countries) know that the organization cared about their personal lives. Davies did so by being open about his own challenges as his wife battled breast cancer, while at the same time helping employees realize that the bank was just as concerned about their emotional and physical health. During his tenure, Davies initiated several programs aimed at boosting employees' overall wellbeing, and he always encouraged his direct reports to put family first. He knew there was no way employees could truly love their organization if it didn't have a heart.

When managers and leaders invest in employees' wellbeing, they are likely to influence organizational growth in the process. When we asked employees the question about whether their manager cares about them as a person, we found that people who agree with this statement:

- are more likely to be top performers

- produce higher quality work

- are less likely to be sick

- are less likely to change jobs

- are less likely to get injured on the job

This all adds up to a more efficient and higher performing organization. Through large-scale studies across more than 150 workplaces, we have found that what's best for the employee isn't at odds with what's best for the organization.

No doubt some leaders will continue to ignore employees' wellbeing as if it is beyond the scope of their jobs, but they do so at their peril. The research we conducted suggests that employees with low engagement and low wellbeing will quickly drag the group's performance down.[*]

---

[*] *For more information on the direct and indirect costs associated with low wellbeing in organizations, e-mail us at wellbeing@gallup.com for a comprehensive paper on the economics of wellbeing in organizations.*

In sharp contrast, the most progressive leaders not only understand that they are in the business of boosting their employees' wellbeing, but they also use this knowledge as a competitive advantage to recruit and retain employees. They know it will be easier to attract top talent if they can show a prospective employee how working for the organization will translate into better relationships, more financial security, improved physical health, and more involvement in the community.

Leaders can't just tell employees that they care about their wellbeing. They have to take action if they want to see results. And this requires continual measurement and follow-up to help workers manage their wellbeing over time. Just as the most successful organizations have worked systemically to optimize their levels of employee engagement, they are now turning their attention to employee wellbeing as a way to gain an emotional, financial, and competitive advantage.

D: Technical Report: The Research and Development of Gallup's Wellbeing Metrics

Purpose

Gallup's goal in developing the Wellbeing Finder was to use current science to create a comprehensive, reliable, valid, concise, and actionable tool that individuals could use to track their wellbeing over time. Our team of scientists sought to identify wellbeing dimensions that explain differences in wellbeing for people in diverse life situations and that represent areas in which individuals can take action to improve their wellbeing. Wellbeing is *all the things that are important to how we think about and experience our lives.*

History of Instrument Design

Development of the Wellbeing Finder occurred in three iterations or phases:

- Phase 1: Review of Historical Gallup Wellbeing Research

- Phase 2: Gallup Global Research and Analysis

- Phase 3: Pilot Research for the Wellbeing Finder Assessment

    Pilot 1: Item testing across diverse groups

    Pilot 2: Refinement of measures/constructs in international samples

Phase 1: Review of Historical Gallup Wellbeing Research

The foundation for the questions in Gallup's Wellbeing Finder is based in the work of George Gallup and his colleagues, which began in the 1930s. In 1960, Dr. Gallup published a study and subsequent book titled *The Secrets of a Long Life*. Gallup research into wellbeing and human needs and satisfaction continued through the 1960s, 1970s, and 1980s.

In the 1990s, Gallup initiated a series of landmark studies. One nationwide study began in China in 1994, long before any other public opinion work was initiated in that country. In 1996, Gallup began a similar nationwide study in India and conducted baseline studies in Israel and the Palestinian Territories in 1999. Also in the 1990s, Gallup conducted several studies of community vitality and satisfaction with life. Between 2001 and 2007, Gallup conducted tens of thousands of interviews with residents of nations that are predominantly Muslim or have substantial Muslim populations. The first truly global research study (representing more than 98% of the world's adult population in more than 150 countries) began in 2005 and continues today.

Many of the question items from past Gallup research are used in or influenced question wording in the Wellbeing Finder. These included questions that measure basic needs such as safety, food, and shelter and higher level needs such as quality of work, health, relationships, economics, and community involvement. Questions were reviewed for evidence of reliability, validity, and applicability to individual intervention (rather than policy-oriented issues).

Phase 2: Gallup Global Research and Analysis

Prior to development of the Gallup global study, thousands of possible questions were considered. The initial pilot survey included 130 items that took respondents 30-35 minutes to complete. This survey was later refined based on statistical analysis to include 100 items that took respondents 20-25 minutes to complete. The seven core indexes assessed are Law and Order, Food and Shelter, Work, Personal Economy, Personal Health, Citizen Engagement, and Wellbeing. The global study now includes substantially more indexes, each of which have been tested for reliability and validity evidence.

Sampling and Data Collection Methodology

With few exceptions, all samples are probability based and nationally representative of the resident population aged 15 and older. The coverage area is the entire country including rural areas, and the sampling frame represents the entire civilian, non-institutionalized, aged 15 and older population of the entire country. Exceptions include areas where the safety of interviewing staff is threatened, scarcely populated islands in some countries, and areas that interviewers can reach only by foot, animal, or small boat.

Telephone surveys are used in countries where telephone coverage represents at least 80% of the population or is the customary survey methodology. In Central and Eastern Europe, as well as in the developing world, including much of Latin America, the former Soviet Union countries, nearly all of Asia, the Middle East, and Africa, an area frame design is used for face-to-face interviewing.

The typical global survey in a country consists of at least 1,000 surveys of individuals. In some large countries, oversamples are collected in major cities or areas of special interest. Although infrequent, there are some instances in which the sample size is between 500 and 1,000.

In addition to the immense coverage of the global study (now more than 98% of the world's population), the concept of wellbeing is considered from a diverse perspective.

Historically, definitions of wellbeing have fallen into two broad categories. The first category consists of traditional neoclassic measures such as income, GDP, life expectancy, and poverty rates. The second includes the subjective or psychological measures of wellbeing that seek to measure how people feel about their lives. Based on more recent research, the second category can be separated into two general types: those measures that tap into the evaluating or remembering self and those that tap into the experiencing self.

Different Measures of Wellbeing

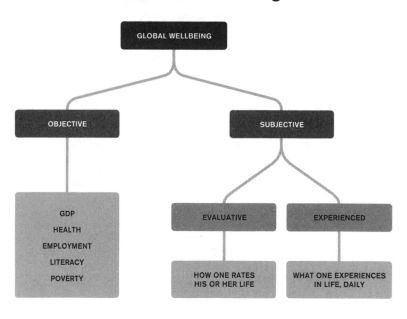

Nobel laureate Daniel Kahneman and University of Illinois at Urbana-Champaign psychology professor Ed Diener have been influential in conceiving the contemporary views of wellbeing. In the journal article "Guidelines for National Indicators of Subjective Well-Being and Ill-Being," Diener defines subjective wellbeing as "all of the various types of evaluations, both positive and negative, that people make of their lives. It includes reflective cognitive evaluations, such as life satisfaction and work satisfaction, interest and engagement, and affective reactions to life events, such as joy and sadness." Similarly, in the book *The Science of Well-Being: Integrating Neurobiology, Psychology, and Social Science*, Kahneman makes note of the distinction between "experienced well-being" and "evaluative well-being." Experienced wellbeing is concerned with momentary affective states and the way people feel about experiences in real time, while evaluative wellbeing is the way they remember their experiences after they are over. Experienced wellbeing seeks to bypass the effects of judgment and memory and has historically been measured using the experience sampling method or the day reconstruction method, both of which seek to capture feelings and emotions as close to the subject's immediate experience as possible.

Inspired by the work of Kahneman and his colleagues, the Gallup global study adapted these methods to a large-scale survey environment by framing a series of experience and emotion questions within the context of the past 24 hours. For example, respondents are asked a series of questions that relate to experiences of positive and negative emotions, including feelings of enjoyment, happiness, stress, and anger. Respondents are also asked whether they felt well-rested the previous day, whether they were treated with respect, smiled or laughed a lot, had a lot of energy, worried about money, and learned or did something interesting. They are also asked about their time use, such as the amount of time spent socially or commuting to work.

Numerous reports and findings from the Gallup global study can be accessed on Gallup.com.

Using our definition of wellbeing as *all the things that are important to how we think about and experience our lives*, we then studied how various elements of wellbeing explained measures of life evaluation/judgment and daily experience.

Phase 3: Pilot Research for the Wellbeing Finder Assessment

Phase 3 began with a review of individual-level data from Gallup's global study. We assessed the generalizability of important key wellbeing domains through regression analysis. Additionally, we reviewed wellbeing literature and conducted qualitative interviews to hypothesize individually actionable areas. Items were written and initially tested between 2004 and 2007. Follow-up pilot testing of the web-based field assessment was conducted between 2007 and 2009.

From this exploratory research, 340 wellbeing items were generated for testing, covering many different life domains and experiences, including: career; interests; passions; life balance; enjoyment of work; satisfaction with boss; stress; purpose; mentors; strengths; family; friends; social time; marriage; children; religion; faith; spirituality; equality; goals; basic needs; housing; income; physical security; financial security; spending habits; peer group; fatigue; diet; exercise; energy; sleep habits; pain; body image; illnesses; sick days; safety; access to food, water, and clean air; community engagement; and contributions to society, in addition to other areas.

Based on exploratory factor analysis, five broad wellbeing dimensions were hypothesized. These dimensions capture the majority of the variance in wellbeing outcome variables such as overall life evaluation in the present, hope for the future, and daily experiences:

- **Career or Occupational Wellbeing:** how people occupy their time during the day and whether it is fulfilling

- **Social Wellbeing:** the quality of relationships in people's lives

- **Financial Wellbeing:** the degree of financial security people have

- **Physical Wellbeing:** the extent to which people can do what they want to do free of pain

- **Community Wellbeing:** the extent to which people feel safe and are involved in giving to their community

As the following chart shows, the 340 items were dispersed across five subsamples and tested for reliability and validity evidence.

Pilot 1: Sample Size by Sample/Subgroups
U.S. Residents – Panel (N=10,544)

CAREER	(N Size) 2,389	COMMUNITY/SAFETY	(N Size) 1,254
Not employed	388	Rural	427
Full-time student	300	Urban	403
Homemaker	386	Suburban	424
Part-time/not full-time student	419	**FINANCIAL**	**(N Size) 2,080**
Retired	473		
Employed full time	423	<$25,000	369
		$25,000 - $49,999	401
PHYSICAL	**(N Size) 2,677**	$50,000 - $99,999	411
HEALTHY	**1,344**	$100,000 - $199,999	429
<50	462	$200,000+	470
50-64	500	**RELATIONSHIP**	**(N Size) 2,144**
65+	382		
UNHEALTHY	**1,333**	Married	436
		Widowed	438
<50	389	Separated/divorced	439
50-64	462	Single/never married	420
65+	482	Living with a partner	411

We oversampled particular subgroups of the Gallup Panel to maximize information on a diverse set of individuals within each wellbeing dimension (people in various career and financial situations; living in assorted locales; and with differing age, health, and relationship status). This allowed us to learn which facets of wellbeing were most important in a variety of contexts. Within each wellbeing dimension, we studied which questions best differentiated those with high versus low wellbeing.

Four primary dependent variables were considered:

1. *Life Evaluation: Present* (0-10 scale)

2. *Life Evaluation: Future* (0-10 scale)

3. *Daily Experiences*: enjoyment, happiness, physical pain, worry, sadness, stress, boredom, anger, contentment

4. *Exceeding Wildest Expectations*: "Up to this point, my life has exceeded my wildest expectations" (1-5 agreement scale)

There were five separate surveys designed for this phase of research (one for each wellbeing dimension). Analysis was conducted within each subsample within each dimension. The goal was to maximize information for each wellbeing dimension by selecting the best items for the next phase of research, considering validity and reliability evidence.

For instance, the Cronbach's alpha reliability exceeded .70 (range of .72 to .91) for each dimension based on retained items, and reliability was consistently high across the subsamples within each dimension. The following table shows the correlations to the four criterion variables for each dimension (the validities did not vary substantially across subsamples).

Pilot 1: Validity Estimates

WELLBEING DIMENSION	LIFE EVALUATION	FUTURE	DAILY EXPERIENCES	WILDEST EXPECTATIONS
Career	0.56	0.47	0.53	0.60
Social	0.54	0.45	0.49	0.55
Financial	0.65	0.48	0.48	0.53
Physical	0.46	0.33	0.46	0.34
Community	0.49	0.37	0.44	0.47

A total of 164 items were retained for the next phase of research, which included a random sample of 2,135 adults aged 18 and older and 172 youths aged 13-17. For this phase of the research, we combined items across wellbeing dimensions to assess the independence of the factors.

The list of items was further refined based on confirmatory factor analysis and further criterion-related validity study, which resulted in 120 items spread across the five wellbeing dimensions. The instrument was then translated into seven languages for further international testing (Chinese-Traditional, Chinese-Simplified, French-European, German, Japanese, Spanish-Latin American, and English-Great Britain).

Factor analysis indicated five distinct factors, each with eigenvalues above 2.0 and each with reliabilities above .75 for adults and youths. The average intercorrelation between dimensions was .51 for adults and .56 for youths. Validity estimates were of similar magnitude to those found in the earlier pilot studies and were generalizable for adults aged 18 and older and youths aged 13-17.

The final field instrument contains 10 items per wellbeing dimension, for a total of 50 scored items plus additional research items.

Pilot 2: Reliability and Validity Estimates

DIMENSION	RELIABILITY	VALIDITY LIFE EVALUATION	FUTURE	DAILY EXPERIENCES	WILDEST EXPECTATIONS	SICK DAYS
Career	0.85	0.58	0.46	0.48	0.60	-0.21
Social	0.86	0.52	0.38	0.45	0.50	-0.12
Financial	0.84	0.63	0.38	0.38	0.51	-0.19
Physical	0.83	0.50	0.37	0.46	0.43	-0.41
Community	0.77	0.38	0.25	0.36	0.40	-0.11

Partial Correlations* With Outcome Variables

WELLBEING DIMENSION	LIFE EVALUATION	FUTURE	DAILY EXPERIENCES	WILDEST EXPECTATIONS	SICK DAYS
Career	0.22	0.18	0.15	0.31	0.00
Social	0.09	0.04	0.09	0.06	0.09
Financial	0.40	0.19	0.13	0.19	0.05
Physical	0.13	0.08	0.24	0.02	0.36
Community	0.00	0.05	0.11	0.08	0.02

*Partial correlations controlling for gender, age, income, education, marital status, employment status, race, and the other four wellbeing dimensions.
Partial correlations in bold have 95% confidence intervals that do not overlap with zero.

Regression analyses were also conducted by first entering demographic variables into the equation (age, gender, employment status, marital status, race, education level, and income level) and then entering each of the wellbeing dimensions. Dependent variables, as previously studied, included *Life Evaluation: Present and Future*, *Daily Experiences*, and *Exceeding Wildest Expectations*. For adults and youths, each dimension accounted for unique information, beyond demographics and other wellbeing dimensions, in multiple dependent variables. For instance, all five dimensions accounted for unique variance in *Daily Experiences*. The first four dimensions (Career, Social, Financial, and Physical) each accounted for unique variance in *Life Evaluation: Future*. The first three dimensions (Career, Social, and Financial) and Community each accounted for unique variance in *Exceeding Wildest Expectations*. Of the five dimensions, the two most highly correlated are Career and Social Wellbeing, correlating .69 for adults and .75 for youths. As such, they may be the most interchangeable in their impact on wellbeing outcomes.

The following table shows the Multiple Rs for demographics and the total model (demographics plus wellbeing dimensions).

Regression: Multiple R

The following are Multiple Rs for demographics and the total model (demographics plus wellbeing dimensions)

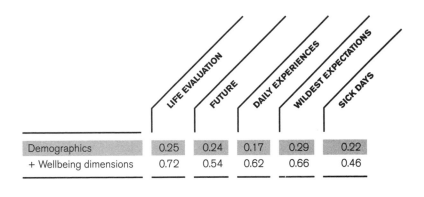

	LIFE EVALUATION	FUTURE	DAILY EXPERIENCES	WILDEST EXPECTATIONS	SICK DAYS
Demographics	0.25	0.24	0.17	0.29	0.22
+ Wellbeing dimensions	0.72	0.54	0.62	0.66	0.46

It is clear that the five wellbeing dimensions, while not explaining all of what makes up a great life for all individuals, describe a great deal across multiple wellbeing outcome variables. They also add substantially to other situational or demographic variables in explaining wellbeing.

After translation into seven languages (Chinese-Traditional [n=829], Chinese-Simplified [n=3,186], French-European [n=288], German [n=522], Japanese [n=3,085], Spanish-Latin American [n=1,210], and English-Great Britain [n=731]), we conducted confirmatory factor analysis and reliability, validity, and generalizability analyses. Based on confirmatory factor analysis, the average item-factor loading ranged from .52 to .58 across the languages. We correlated the item-factor loadings across languages, and the strength of the individual item-factor loadings was very similar across languages (mean r of 50 item-factor loadings across languages=.79). SRMR (standardized root mean squared residual) fit ranged from .06 to .071 across languages, indicating acceptable fit of the factor model to the data. The mean item-dimension corrected correlation (corrected for part-whole overlap) was 50% higher than the mean item correlation to other dimensions. Additionally, the pattern of intercorrelations among dimensions (that is, how dimensions related to each other) was similar across languages. (The correlation matrices agreed across languages; mean r=.89.) The reliability of the dimensions was also similar across languages.

Mean Reliability Across Languages

WELLBEING DIMENSION	MEAN RELIABILITY
Career	0.86
Social	0.85
Financial	0.75
Physical	0.77
Community	0.72
Overall	0.93

We also conducted meta-analysis to understand the generalizability of each wellbeing dimension's relationship to each of the criterion variables across languages. The correlation of each dimension to *Life Evaluation: Future, Daily Experiences, Exceeding Wildest Expectations,* and sick days was in the hypothesized direction and generalizable across languages.

Daily Experience Tracker

Based on the same series of iterative research studies as previously outlined, we sought to define a core set of items that could be asked daily to help individuals track their "experiencing self" more frequently and learn from their best and worst days. The following 10 conditions are included in the daily wellbeing assessment:

1. Feeling well-rested

2. Being treated with respect

3. Smiling or laughter

4. Learning or interest

5. Enjoyment

6. Physical pain

7. Worry

8. Sadness

9. Stress

10. Anger

These 10 conditions don't explain everything that makes up a good day, but rather they measure the core elements of a good day for most people in the world. The 10-item scale results in a score of 0-10 for each person, each day. We conducted reliability and validity studies in more than 140 countries to assess the scale's appropriateness cross-culturally.

Of the individuals we randomly surveyed, those scoring a perfect 10 were 94% likely to say "yes" they "would like to have more days just like yesterday." The following table shows the probability of people saying "yes" they "would like to have more days like yesterday" for scores from 0-10.

Days Like Yesterday

The probability of "yes" to "I would like to have more days just like yesterday" (n = 147,695)

SCORE	PROBABILITY
10	94%
9	88%
8	80%
7	70%
6	57%
5	43%
4	31%
3	21%
2	13%
1	8%
0	4%

The Cronbach's alpha reliability of the scale is .73 for respondents across all countries (mean within-country reliability=.73, s=.07).

Across the seven language samples used for cross-validation on the web assessment, the mean reliability of the 10-item scale was .82 (s=.03).

We conducted a meta-analysis of the relationship between the *Daily Experiences* total score and the dependent variable (I would like to have more days just like yesterday; yes=1, no=0). The mean observed correlation across countries was .54 (s=.10). Correcting for range variation and reliability of the independent variable, the estimated true score correlation between the *Daily Experience* 0-10 total score and the dichotomous dependent variable was .73 (SDρ=.07; 90% Credibility Value=.64). The meta-analytic true score correlation has not yet been corrected for dependent variable measurement error, and it is thus biased downward. The reliability and criterion-related validity of the 10-item scale is high and generalizable across countries.

Summary

The Gallup Wellbeing Finder was developed based on a foundation of world research and a history of studying wellbeing. The tool is our best attempt to summarize what makes most people's lives and days fulfilling. The Wellbeing Finder is designed to create awareness of measureable and actionable issues. While a great deal has gone into the science of the Wellbeing Finder to date, future research will provide substantial insight into how it is most effectively applied and how measurement can be continually refined to provide the best insights, with the goal to improve the wellbeing of the world's citizens.

E: The Five Essential Elements: Definitions

CAREER WELLBEING

Many of us work in a traditional organizational setting, while others work in homes, classrooms, factories, or outdoors. Some of us are retirees or volunteers. No matter where we spend our time, at a basic level, we need something to do — and ideally something to look forward to. Career Wellbeing is about liking what you do every day.

People with high Career Wellbeing wake up every morning with something to look forward to doing that day. They also have the opportunity to do things that fit their strengths and interests. They have a deep purpose in life and a plan to attain their goals. In most cases, they have a leader who motivates them and makes them enthusiastic about the future and friends who share their passion.

While you might think that people with high Career Wellbeing spend too much time working at the expense of their relationships, our results suggest that they actually take more time to enjoy life and don't take things for granted. This results in them loving the work they do every day.

SOCIAL WELLBEING

We often underestimate the impact of our closest relationships and social connections on our wellbeing. However, our wellbeing is dramatically influenced by the people around us as well as by our friends' independent network of relationships. Some of these friendships help us to achieve, while others motivate us to be healthy. Social Wellbeing is about having strong relationships and love in your life.

People with high Social Wellbeing have several close relationships that help them achieve, enjoy life, and be healthy. They are surrounded by people who encourage their development and growth, accept them for who they are, and treat them with respect. They deliberately spend time investing in the networks that surround them.

People with high Social Wellbeing are more likely to make time for vacations or social gatherings with their friends and family, and that strengthens their relationships. They report having a great deal of love in their lives, and this gives them positive energy on a daily basis.

FINANCIAL WELLBEING

Money may not buy happiness, but it is hard to be happy if you cannot meet your basic needs. Beyond that, the actual amount of money you have has less of an impact on your overall wellbeing than financial security and how you manage and spend your money. Financial Wellbeing is about effectively managing your economic life.

People with high Financial Wellbeing manage their personal finances well and spend their money wisely. They buy experiences instead of just material possessions, and they give to others instead of always spending on themselves. At a basic level, they are satisfied with their overall standard of living.

Their successful strategies result in financial security, which eliminates daily stress and worry caused by debt. This financial security allows them to do what they want to do when they want to do it. They have the freedom to spend more time with the people they like to be around.

PHYSICAL WELLBEING

The short-term choices we make can have a long-term effect on our overall physical health. When we adopt healthy habits and make smart lifestyle choices about diet, exercise, and sleep, we feel better, have more energy, look better, and live longer. Physical Wellbeing is about having good health and enough energy to get things done on a daily basis.

People with high Physical Wellbeing manage their health well. They exercise regularly, and as a result, they feel better. They make good dietary choices, which keeps their energy high throughout the day and sharpens their thinking. They get enough sleep to process what they have learned the day before and to get a good start on the next day.

Because of their healthy lifestyle, they are usually able to do all the things people their age would normally do. When they wake up well-rested each day, they look better, feel better, and have more energy.

COMMUNITY WELLBEING

At a basic level, we need to feel safe where we live and secure about the quality of the water we drink and the air we breathe. We also need to have a home that meets our needs and a community we can take pride in. When we get involved in our community and give back to society, it benefits us as well as the recipients and our entire community. This "well-doing" promotes deeper social interaction, enhanced meaning and purpose, and a more active lifestyle. Community Wellbeing is about the sense of engagement you have with the area where you live.

People with high Community Wellbeing feel safe and secure where they live. They take pride in their community and feel that it's headed in the right direction. This often results in their wanting to give back and make a lasting contribution to society. These people have identified the areas where they can contribute based on their own strengths and passions, and they tell others about these interests to connect with the right groups and causes.

Their contributions to the community may start small, but over time, they lead to more involvement and have a profound impact on the community in which they live. These efforts are what create communities we cannot imagine living without. The positive outcomes of high Community Wellbeing may be what differentiates a good life from a great one.

F: Wellbeing Across the United States

Wellbeing: U.S. States

Sorted by percentage thriving

⤴ % Thriving	〰 % Struggling	❗ % Suffering

RANK	STATE	⤴	〰	❗	DAILY EXPERIENCE
1	Hawaii	56.2	40.4	3.5	8.0
2	Alaska	54.9	42.5	2.5	7.9
3	Maryland	54.6	42.3	3.1	7.7
4	Utah	54.2	43.4	2.4	7.6
5	Virginia	52.8	44.0	3.1	7.7
6	Colorado	52.5	44.4	3.1	7.6
7	Georgia	52.3	44.2	3.5	7.6
8	Texas	52.1	44.6	3.3	7.6
9	Montana	51.5	45.0	3.5	7.8
10	New Mexico	51.5	44.6	4.0	7.5
11	Washington	51.1	45.2	3.7	7.6
12	Minnesota	50.9	45.2	3.9	7.9
13	California	50.7	45.9	3.4	7.5
14	Louisiana	50.5	45.9	3.7	7.6
15	Kansas	50.4	46.2	3.4	7.8
16	Idaho	50.4	45.5	4.1	7.6
17	Delaware	50.3	45.8	3.9	7.6
18	Oregon	50.1	45.5	4.4	7.6
19	Massachusetts	50.1	46.6	3.4	7.5
20	South Dakota	49.9	45.6	4.5	7.8
21	Arizona	49.8	47.0	3.2	7.6
22	Illinois	49.8	47.2	3.0	7.7
23	New Jersey	49.6	46.7	3.7	7.5
24	North Dakota	49.5	46.6	3.9	8.1
25	Connecticut	49.2	47.0	3.7	7.5
26	New York	49.0	47.4	3.6	7.5
27	New Hampshire	49.0	46.7	4.4	7.6

Source: Gallup-Healthways Well-Being Index (January-December 2009)

Wellbeing: U.S. States (cont'd)

Sorted by percentage thriving

 % Thriving    **% Struggling**   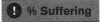 **% Suffering**

RANK	STATE			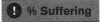	DAILY EXPERIENCE
28	Iowa	48.8	47.8	3.4	7.9
29	Nebraska	48.5	47.9	3.6	7.7
30	North Carolina	48.5	47.2	4.3	7.6
31	Maine	48.5	47.2	4.3	7.6
32	Oklahoma	48.4	48.0	3.6	7.5
33	Vermont	48.2	45.7	6.1	7.7
34	Mississippi	48.2	47.0	4.8	7.6
35	South Carolina	48.0	47.5	4.5	7.7
36	Alabama	47.8	48.0	4.2	7.5
37	Michigan	47.6	48.1	4.4	7.6
38	Missouri	47.4	48.4	4.2	7.6
39	Tennessee	47.4	47.8	4.8	7.4
40	Florida	47.4	48.5	4.1	7.5
41	Pennsylvania	47.2	48.6	4.2	7.6
42	Wyoming	46.8	49.6	3.6	7.8
43	Indiana	46.5	49.2	4.4	7.5
44	Ohio	46.2	49.3	4.6	7.4
45	Wisconsin	45.7	50.1	4.2	7.8
46	Kentucky	45.6	49.2	5.2	7.3
47	Nevada	45.4	49.6	5.0	7.5
48	Rhode Island	45.3	51.6	3.1	7.4
49	Arkansas	44.7	50.2	5.1	7.4
50	West Virginia	43.2	50.4	6.4	7.2

Source: Gallup-Healthways Well-Being Index (January-December 2009)

Wellbeing: U.S. Cities
Sorted by percentage thriving

 % Thriving    **% Struggling**   **% Suffering**

Large (Population: 1,000,000+)

RANK	CITY				DAILY EXPERIENCE
1	Washington/Arlington/Alexandria, D.C./VA/MD/WV	58.7	39.0	2.3	7.8
2	Charlotte/Gastonia/Concord, NC/SC	55.5	41.7	2.8	7.7
3	San Antonio, TX	55.3	41.8	2.8	7.6
4	Atlanta/Sandy Springs/Marietta, GA	55.1	42.0	2.8	7.7
5	Virginia Beach/Norfolk/Newport News, VA/NC	55.1	42.8	2.2	7.8
6	Austin/Round Rock, TX	54.8	39.5	5.7	7.8
7	Kansas City, MO/KS	54.8	42.6	2.7	7.7
8	Dallas/Fort Worth/Arlington, TX	53.6	43.5	2.9	7.7
9	Raleigh/Cary, NC	53.6	42.4	4.0	7.7
10	San Francisco/Oakland/Fremont, CA	53.5	43.8	2.7	7.6
11	Seattle/Tacoma/Bellevue, WA	53.3	43.9	2.8	7.6
12	Memphis, TN/MS/AR	53.2	43.4	3.4	7.6
13	Nashville/Davidson/Murfreesboro/ Franklin, TN	52.8	43.8	3.4	7.7
14	Houston/Sugar Land/Baytown, TX	52.5	44.6	2.9	7.7
15	Minneapolis/St. Paul/Bloomington, MN/WI	52.4	44.3	3.2	7.9
16	San Jose/Sunnyvale/Santa Clara, CA	52.2	45.8	2.0	7.7
17	Riverside/San Bernardino/Ontario, CA	52.1	44.9	2.9	7.5
18	Portland/Vancouver/Beaverton, OR/WA	52.1	44.0	3.9	7.6
19	Denver/Aurora, CO	51.8	45.3	2.9	7.5
20	Boston/Cambridge/Quincy, MA/NH	51.5	45.7	2.9	7.6
21	San Diego/Carlsbad/San Marcos, CA	50.9	45.8	3.3	7.7
22	Los Angeles/Long Beach/Santa Ana, CA	50.9	45.9	3.2	7.5

Source: Gallup-Healthways Well-Being Index (January-December 2009)

Wellbeing: U.S. Cities (cont'd)

Sorted by percentage thriving

 % Thriving    % Struggling   **❶ % Suffering**

Large (Population: 1,000,000+)

RANK	CITY	➶	⩗	❶	DAILY EXPERIENCE
23	Oklahoma City, OK	50.6	46.3	3.1	7.6
24	Philadelphia/Camden/Wilmington, PA/NJ/DE/MD	50.6	46.1	3.3	7.5
25	Buffalo/Niagara Falls, NY	50.5	45.7	3.7	7.4
26	Orlando/Kissimmee, FL	50.3	47.0	2.7	7.6
27	Phoenix/Mesa/Scottsdale, AZ	50.1	46.8	3.0	7.6
28	Indianapolis/Carmel, IN	50.1	45.7	4.2	7.6
29	New York/Northern New Jersey/Long Island, NY/NJ/PA	49.9	46.8	3.3	7.4
30	Jacksonville, FL	49.8	45.2	5.0	7.4
31	New Orleans/Metairie/Kenner, LA	49.8	46.2	4.0	7.5
32	Hartford/West Hartford/East Hartford, CT	49.7	46.8	3.5	7.6
33	Columbus, OH	49.7	46.7	3.6	7.5
34	Salt Lake City, UT	49.6	48.2	2.2	7.5
35	Sacramento/Arden-Arcade/Roseville, CA	49.5	46.9	3.6	7.6
36	St. Louis, MO/IL	49.5	47.6	3.0	7.7
37	Cleveland/Elyria/Mentor, OH	48.9	47.1	4.0	7.6
38	Miami/Fort Lauderdale/Pompano Beach, FL	48.6	47.7	3.8	7.4
39	Louisville/Jefferson County, KY/IN	48.1	48.5	3.4	7.6
40	Chicago/Naperville/Joliet, IL/IN/WI	47.7	48.2	4.1	7.3
41	Rochester, NY	47.6	48.4	4.0	7.6
42	Cincinnati/Middletown, OH/KY/IN	47.5	48.5	4.0	7.5
43	Pittsburgh, PA	47.3	48.4	4.3	7.6
44	Baltimore/Towson, MD	47.1	49.4	3.5	7.3
45	Detroit/Warren/Livonia, MI	46.3	49.4	4.2	7.5

Source: Gallup-Healthways Well-Being Index (January-December 2009)

Wellbeing: U.S. Cities (cont'd)

Sorted by percentage thriving

  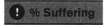

Large (Population: 1,000,000+)

RANK	CITY	↗	⌁	!	DAILY EXPERIENCE
46	Worcester, MA	46.2	49.8	4.1	7.4
47	Milwaukee/Waukesha/West Allis, WI	45.3	51.8	2.9	7.7
48	Las Vegas/Paradise, NV	45.2	50.2	4.6	7.4
49	Providence/New Bedford/Fall River, RI/MA	45.0	51.5	3.5	7.4
50	Tampa/St. Petersburg/Clearwater, FL	44.7	50.9	4.4	7.5
51	Cincinnati/Middletown, OH/KY/IN	41.9	52.7	5.4	7.3

Source: Gallup-Healthways Well-Being Index (January–December 2009)

Wellbeing: U.S. Cities

Sorted by percentage thriving

Midsized (Population: 999,000-250,000)

RANK	CITY	⬈	⌇	❗	DAILY EXPERIENCE
1	Beaumont/Port Arthur, TX	60.9	37.1	2.0	7.7
2	Killeen/Temple/Fort Hood, TX	60.3	37.8	1.9	7.9
3	Bradenton/Sarasota/Venice, FL	60.2	36.1	3.7	7.8
4	Provo/Orem, UT	59.8	38.8	1.5	7.9
5	Bridgeport/Stamford/Norwalk, CT	59.6	37.8	2.6	7.9
6	Ann Arbor, MI	59.1	38.2	2.7	7.8
7	Honolulu, HI	57.6	38.9	3.5	8.1
8	Holland/Grand Haven, MI	56.9	41.3	1.8	8.1
9	Tallahassee, FL	56.5	40.5	3.0	7.4
10	Bakersfield, CA	56.4	40.6	3.0	7.7
11	Ogden/Clearfield, UT	56.0	40.8	3.2	7.4
12	Colorado Springs, CO	55.6	41.2	3.2	7.6
13	Anchorage, AK	55.5	42.1	2.4	7.9
14	McAllen/Edinburg/Mission, TX	55.0	43.2	1.8	7.6
15	Lexington/Fayette, KY	54.9	42.7	2.4	7.7
16	Santa Barbara/Santa Maria/Goleta, CA	54.2	42.6	3.2	7.6
17	Huntsville, AL	54.1	42.7	3.1	7.7
18	Santa Rosa/Petaluma, CA	54.0	42.8	3.2	7.7
19	Naples/Marco Island, FL	54.0	43.5	2.5	7.9
20	Norwich/New London, CT	53.8	43.9	2.3	7.8
21	Tucson, AZ	53.5	43.7	2.7	7.6
22	El Paso, TX	53.3	44.8	1.9	7.7
23	Trenton/Ewing, NJ	53.2	45.5	1.2	7.6
24	Durham, NC	52.9	43.2	3.9	7.8
25	Corpus Christi, TX	52.9	43.5	3.6	7.5
26	Albuquerque, NM	52.9	44.5	2.6	7.6

Source: Gallup-Healthways Well-Being Index (January-December 2009)

Wellbeing: U.S. Cities (cont'd)

Sorted by percentage thriving

 % Thriving 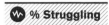 **% Struggling** 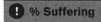 **% Suffering**

Midsized (Population: 999,000-250,000)

RANK	CITY		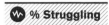	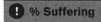	DAILY EXPERIENCE
27	Fayetteville, Springdale/Rogers, AR/MO	52.6	43.4	3.9	7.5
28	Grand Rapids/Wyoming, MI	52.6	43.4	4.0	7.6
29	Lansing/East Lansing, MI	52.5	41.8	5.7	7.6
30	Charleston, WV	52.3	45.2	2.5	8.1
31	Oxnard/Thousand Oaks/Ventura, CA	52.3	43.8	4.0	7.6
32	Chattanooga, TN/GA	52.1	45.0	2.9	7.6
33	Boulder, CO	51.8	44.9	3.3	7.6
34	South Bend/Mishawaka, IN/MI	51.8	44.0	4.3	7.4
35	Birmingham/Hoover, AL	51.7	45.3	2.9	7.9
36	Madison, WI	51.6	44.2	4.2	7.7
37	Salinas, CA	51.5	45.2	3.3	7.5
38	Columbia, SC	51.5	44.6	3.9	7.8
39	Binghamton, NY	51.4	45.4	3.2	7.5
40	Mobile, AL	51.4	44.7	3.9	7.6
41	Baton Rouge, LA	51.4	44.8	3.8	7.6
42	Fayetteville, NC	51.2	46.2	2.6	7.6
43	Eugene/Springfield, OR	51.2	45.2	3.6	7.7
44	Santa Cruz/Watsonville, CA	51.0	45.4	3.6	7.7
45	Omaha/Council Bluffs, NE/IA	50.7	46.7	2.6	7.7
46	Salem, OR	50.7	45.1	4.2	7.9
47	Vallejo/Fairfield, CA	50.7	43.5	5.8	7.5
48	Des Moines/West Des Moines, IA	50.6	47.7	1.7	7.8
49	Fort Collins/Loveland, CO	50.5	46.9	2.6	7.5
50	Fresno, CA	50.5	46.0	3.5	7.4
51	Albany/Schenectady/Troy, NY	50.3	46.0	3.7	7.6
52	Peoria, IL	50.3	45.2	4.5	7.8

Source: Gallup-Healthways Well-Being Index (January-December 2009)

Wellbeing: U.S. Cities (cont'd)

Sorted by percentage thriving

Midsized (Population: 999,000-250,000)

RANK	CITY	↗	⌁	!	DAILY EXPERIENCE
53	Wichita, KS	50.2	46.7	3.1	7.8
54	Davenport/Moline/Rock Island, IA/IL	50.1	46.2	3.7	7.9
55	Boise City/Nampa, ID	49.8	46.3	3.9	7.7
56	Lancaster, PA	49.7	47.2	3.1	7.8
57	Knoxville, TN	49.5	46.3	4.3	7.5
58	Richmond, VA	49.3	47.1	3.6	7.7
59	Little Rock/North Little Rock/Conway, AR	49.3	47.8	3.0	7.6
60	Augusta/Richmond County, GA/SC	49.1	47.5	3.4	7.6
61	Ocala, FL	48.9	48.0	3.1	7.6
62	Dayton, OH	48.8	46.8	4.4	7.5
63	Palm Bay/Melbourne/Titusville, FL	48.8	46.8	4.4	7.4
64	Erie, PA	48.6	47.2	4.2	7.5
65	Kalamazoo/Portage, MI	48.5	47.0	4.4	7.7
66	Springfield, MA	48.5	47.6	3.9	7.4
67	Canton/Massillon, OH	48.4	45.6	6.1	7.8
68	Greenville/Mauldin/Easley, SC	48.4	48.0	3.6	7.6
69	Harrisburg/Carlisle, PA	48.3	49.0	2.7	7.6
70	Allentown/Bethlehem/Easton, PA/NJ	48.3	47.7	3.9	7.5
71	Rockford, IL	48.2	48.9	2.8	7.5
72	Winston-Salem, NC	48.2	47.9	3.9	7.7
73	Greensboro/High Point, NC	48.1	47.9	4.0	7.5
74	Syracuse, NY	47.8	49.5	2.7	7.4
75	Shreveport/Bossier City, LA	47.7	46.0	6.3	7.7
76	Hagerstown/Martinsburg, MD/WV	47.6	44.6	7.8	7.2
77	Tulsa, OK	47.6	49.5	2.9	7.5
78	Reading, PA	47.2	46.2	6.6	7.6

Source: Gallup-Healthways Well-Being Index (January-December 2009)

Wellbeing: U.S. Cities (cont'd)

Sorted by percentage thriving

 % Thriving    **% Struggling**   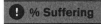 **% Suffering**

Midsized (Population: 999,000-250,000)

RANK	CITY	↗	ᴍᴡ	!	DAILY EXPERIENCE
79	Visalia/Porterville, CA	46.8	48.6	4.6	7.5
80	Springfield, MO	46.7	49.2	4.2	7.5
81	Pensacola/Ferry Pass/Brent, FL	46.6	48.9	4.5	7.3
82	Spokane, WA	46.0	50.4	3.5	7.5
83	Akron, OH	46.0	49.8	4.2	7.6
84	New Haven/Milford, CT	46.0	50.3	3.7	7.4
85	Manchester/Nashua, NH	46.0	49.1	4.9	7.5
86	Savannah, GA	45.9	51.0	3.1	7.4
87	Reno/Sparks, NV	45.7	49.4	4.9	7.3
88	Cape Coral/Fort Myers, FL	45.6	48.4	6.1	7.5
89	Huntington/Ashland, WV/KY/OH	45.5	45.6	8.9	7.1
90	Lakeland/Winter Haven, FL	45.0	50.6	4.4	7.6
91	Evansville, IN/KY	44.7	50.3	5.0	7.3
92	Poughkeepsie/Newburgh/Middletown, NY	44.4	52.0	3.6	7.2
93	Utica/Rome, NY	44.2	50.5	5.2	7.5
94	Montgomery, AL	44.2	52.1	3.8	7.6
95	Scranton/Wilkes-Barre, PA	43.6	51.7	4.7	7.5
96	Fort Wayne, IN	43.6	53.1	3.3	7.6
97	Modesto, CA	43.6	49.1	7.3	7.0
98	Deltona/Daytona Beach/Ormond Beach, FL	43.5	52.8	3.7	7.6
99	Charleston/North Charleston/ Summerville, SC	43.3	53.2	3.6	7.1
100	Toledo, OH	42.8	53.3	3.9	7.6
101	York/Hanover, PA	42.6	54.2	3.2	7.6
102	Youngstown/Warren/Boardman, OH/PA	42.3	51.2	6.5	7.3

Source: Gallup-Healthways Well-Being Index (January-December 2009)

Wellbeing: U.S. Cities (cont'd)
Sorted by percentage thriving

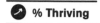  

Midsized (Population: 999,000-250,000)

RANK	CITY	➷	⌇	❗	DAILY EXPERIENCE
103	Flint, MI	41.8	53.1	5.2	7.4
104	Port St. Lucie, FL	41.6	54.6	3.7	7.7
105	Hickory/Lenoir/Morganton, NC	41.2	50.2	8.6	7.1
106	Stockton, CA	40.5	55.5	4.0	7.4
107	Kingsport/Bristol, TN/VA	39.2	54.6	6.2	7.3

Source: Gallup-Healthways Well-Being Index (January-December 2009)

Wellbeing: U.S. Cities
Sorted by percentage thriving

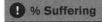

⊘ % Thriving   **〰 % Struggling**   **❗ % Suffering**

Small (Population: Less Than 250,000)

RANK	CITY	⊘	〰	❗	DAILY EXPERIENCE
1	Gainesville, FL	58.4	38.9	2.7	7.6
2	Bangor, ME	54.5	42.3	3.1	7.7
3	Jackson, MS	54.2	42.4	3.4	7.9
4	Yakima, WA	53.3	43.2	3.5	7.5
5	Portland/South Portland/Biddeford, ME	52.7	44.5	2.8	7.6
6	San Luis Obispo/Paso Robles, CA	52.3	44.3	3.4	7.6
7	Wilmington, NC	52.3	45.4	2.3	7.7
8	Bellingham, WA	51.5	45.0	3.5	7.6
9	Chico, CA	51.1	46.4	2.5	7.6
10	Olympia, WA	51.0	44.5	4.4	7.6
11	Lincoln, NE	50.9	46.7	2.3	7.6
12	Kennewick/Pasco/Richland, WA	50.2	46.7	3.1	7.7
13	Lynchburg, VA	49.5	47.6	2.9	7.5
14	Barnstable Town, MA	48.7	47.5	3.8	7.8
15	Medford, OR	48.6	46.6	4.8	7.5
16	Asheville, NC	47.9	47.4	4.7	7.6
17	Burlington/South Burlington, VT	47.8	47.8	4.4	7.5
18	Green Bay, WI	45.6	50.2	4.2	7.7
19	Bremerton/Silverdale, WA	45.3	49.7	5.0	7.8
20	Prescott, AZ	45.0	49.9	5.1	7.9
21	Roanoke, VA	44.4	52.0	3.6	7.6
22	Duluth, MN/WI	44.1	51.3	4.6	7.9
23	Cedar Rapids, IA	42.9	51.1	6.0	7.5
24	Myrtle Beach/North Myrtle Beach/Conway, SC	42.3	50.7	7.0	7.9
25	Topeka, KS	41.8	54.9	3.3	7.4

Source: Gallup-Healthways Well-Being Index (January-December 2009)

Wellbeing: U.S. Cities (cont'd)

Sorted by percentage thriving

📈 % Thriving	〰 % Struggling	❗ % Suffering

Small (Population: Less Than 250,000)

RANK	CITY	📈	〰	❗	DAILY EXPERIENCE
26	Redding, CA	41.5	53.8	4.7	7.5
27	Fort Smith, AR/OK	38.2	57.0	4.8	7.0
28	Lake Havasu City/Kingman, AZ	38.1	57.2	4.7	7.4
29	Johnstown, PA	35.2	57.8	7.0	7.2

Source: Gallup-Healthways Well-Being Index (January-December 2009)

U.S. State and City Wellbeing: Methodology

Percentages of residents who are "thriving," "struggling," and "suffering" for states and cities (in the United States) were derived based on how people evaluated their lives on the Cantril Self-Anchoring Striving Scale. The tables also provide daily wellbeing averages (0-10 scoring) based on responses to 10 items measuring daily experiences (feeling well-rested, being treated with respect, smiling/laughter, learning/interest, enjoyment, physical pain, worry, sadness, stress, and anger). Each daily experience is scored dichotomously with higher scores representing better days (more positive and less negative daily experience or affect).

The survey methods for Gallup-Healthways Well-Being Index rely on live (not automated) interviewers, dual-frame random-digit-dial sampling (which includes landlines as well as wireless phone sampling to reach those in wireless-only households), and a random selection method for choosing respondents within a household. Additionally, daily tracking includes Spanish-language interviews for respondents who speak only Spanish, includes interviews in Alaska and Hawaii, and relies on a multi-call design to reach respondents not contacted on the initial attempt. The data are weighted daily to compensate for disproportionalities in selection probabilities and nonresponse. The data are weighted to match targets from the U.S. Census Bureau by age, sex, region, gender, education, ethnicity, and race.

With the inclusion of the cell phone-only households and the Spanish language interviews, 98% of the adult population is represented in the sample. By comparison, typical landline-only methodologies represent approximately 85% of the adult population.

For this book, 353,849 interviews were aggregated from January 2, 2009-December 30, 2009, among national adults aged 18 and older. Sample sizes vary for states and cities, depending on sample coverage and population sizes (the minimum sample size criterion of approximately 300 was used, although nearly all states and city estimates are based on much larger sample sizes, with a median sample size of 676 for cities and 4,927 for states). For results based on a sample size of 5,000, one can say with 95% confidence that the maximum margin of sampling error is ±1.4 percentage points. For results based on a sample size of 1,000, the maximum margin of sampling error is ±3.1 percentage points; for results based on 500, ±4.4 percentage points; and for results based on 300, ±5.7 percentage points.

In addition to sampling error, question wording and practical difficulties in conducting surveys can introduce error or bias into the findings of public opinion polls.

G: Wellbeing Around the World

Wellbeing: Countries and Areas

Sorted by percentage thriving

⟋ % Thriving   **〰 % Struggling**   **❗ % Suffering**

RANK	COUNTRY	⟋	〰	❗	DAILY EXPERIENCE
1	Denmark	82	17	1	7.9
2	Finland	75	23	2	7.8
3	Ireland	72	28	0	8.1
4	Norway	69	31	0	7.9
5	Sweden	68	30	2	7.9
6	Netherlands	68	32	1	7.7
7	Canada	68	31	1	7.8
8	New Zealand	63	35	2	7.6
9	Switzerland	62	36	2	7.6
10	Australia	62	35	3	7.5
11	Spain	60	37	3	7.3
12	Israel	60	36	4	6.4
13	Austria	57	40	3	7.7
14	United Kingdom	56	41	3	7.4
15	Belgium	56	41	3	7.3
16	Mexico	52	44	4	7.8
17	Panama	51	46	2	8.2
18	United Arab Emirates	51	46	3	7.2
19	United States	50	47	4	7.6
20	France	49	49	2	7.0
21	Saudi Arabia	48	51	1	6.8
22	Puerto Rico	47	45	8	7.6
23	Jamaica	46	49	5	7.7
24	Singapore	46	49	5	7.0
25	Kuwait	45	54	1	7.5
26	Trinidad and Tobago	44	51	5	7.9
27	Colombia	44	48	7	7.4

Source: Gallup World Poll 2005-2009

Wellbeing: Countries and Areas (cont'd)

Sorted by percentage thriving

 % Thriving  % Struggling 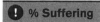 % Suffering

RANK	COUNTRY	⬈	〰	❗	DAILY EXPERIENCE
28	Greece	44	49	7	7.1
29	Belize	44	50	6	6.8
30	Italy	42	52	6	6.7
31	Venezuela	42	52	6	8.0
32	Costa Rica	40	54	6	7.9
33	Cyprus	40	53	7	7.0
34	Czech Republic	39	51	9	6.6
35	Kazakhstan	39	57	4	6.9
36	Brazil	37	57	6	7.4
37	Germany	36	56	7	7.3
38	Argentina	33	58	8	7.2
39	Guatemala	33	59	8	7.8
40	Chile	32	56	12	7.0
41	Guyana	31	64	5	7.0
42	Russia	31	56	13	7.1
43	Uruguay	31	58	11	7.3
44	Lithuania	29	55	16	6.1
45	Kosovo	29	65	6	6.2
46	Poland	28	61	10	7.1
47	Slovenia	28	58	13	7.0
48	Dominican Republic	28	53	19	6.8
49	Pakistan	27	50	23	6.2
50	Honduras	26	59	14	7.7
51	Belarus	26	63	11	7.0
52	Malaysia	25	69	6	7.7
53	Japan	25	65	11	7.4
54	Botswana	24	65	11	7.3

Source: Gallup World Poll 2005-2009

Wellbeing: Countries and Areas (cont'd)

Sorted by percentage thriving

 % Thriving  % Struggling % Suffering

RANK	COUNTRY				DAILY EXPERIENCE
55	South Korea	24	61	15	6.5
56	Cuba	24	66	11	6.7
57	Peru	23	56	20	6.9
58	Lebanon	23	60	17	5.8
59	Ecuador	22	62	15	7.6
60	Thailand	22	72	6	7.8
61	Algeria	22	71	7	6.2
62	Portugal	22	61	17	7.1
63	Taiwan	22	64	14	7.5
64	Nicaragua	21	56	23	7.4
65	Romania	21	56	23	6.6
66	South Africa	21	71	8	7.3
67	Bolivia	21	69	10	6.9
68	Slovakia	21	60	19	6.5
69	Azerbaijan	21	65	14	6.4
70	Estonia	20	64	16	7.0
71	Uzbekistan	20	74	5	7.6
72	Ukraine	20	58	22	6.7
73	Iran	19	66	14	6.3
74	Tajikistan	19	74	7	6.6
75	India	19	74	7	6.5
76	Indonesia	18	72	10	8.2
77	Turkey	18	62	20	6.1
78	Latvia	18	62	20	7.0
79	Vietnam	17	77	5	7.2
80	Tunisia	17	77	6	6.8
81	El Salvador	16	56	28	7.8

Source: Gallup World Poll 2005-2009

Wellbeing: Countries and Areas (cont'd)
Sorted by percentage thriving

 % Thriving  **% Struggling**   **% Suffering**

RANK	COUNTRY	⊘	⌁	!	DAILY EXPERIENCE
82	Ghana	16	79	5	7.6
83	Egypt	16	71	14	6.4
84	Bangladesh	16	71	13	6.9
85	Hong Kong	15	71	14	6.8
86	Nigeria	14	83	3	7.2
87	Cameroon	14	77	9	7.0
88	Malawi	14	79	7	7.5
89	Zambia	14	78	8	7.6
90	Hungary	13	53	34	6.9
91	China	13	77	10	7.8
92	Philippines	13	70	18	6.7
93	Central African Republic	12	75	13	6.4
94	Armenia	12	74	14	6.2
95	Sudan	12	78	10	7.1
96	Kyrgyzstan	12	75	14	7.3
97	Namibia	11	79	10	8.1
98	Palestinian Territories	11	68	21	5.5
99	Angola	11	81	8	6.8
100	Morocco	11	82	8	7.7
101	Mozambique	10	78	11	7.2
102	Sri Lanka	10	76	15	7.1
103	Georgia	10	56	35	6.2
104	Kenya	9	78	13	7.5
105	Rwanda	8	77	15	6.9
106	Guinea	8	89	3	7.1
107	Mongolia	7	81	12	7.0
108	Senegal	7	87	6	7.2

Source: Gallup World Poll 2005-2009

Wellbeing: Countries and Areas (cont'd)

Sorted by percentage thriving

 % Thriving  % Struggling % Suffering

RANK	COUNTRY				DAILY EXPERIENCE
109	Nepal	7	82	11	7.4
110	Madagascar	7	84	10	7.0
111	Uganda	6	71	23	6.8
112	Tanzania	6	70	24	7.5
113	Bulgaria	6	58	36	6.5
114	Ethiopia	5	65	29	7.0
115	Chad	5	88	7	7.1
116	Liberia	5	90	5	6.7
117	Afghanistan	5	68	27	6.1
118	Congo (Kinshasa)	5	83	12	6.8
119	Mauritania	5	82	13	7.3
120	Haiti	4	60	35	6.2
121	Cambodia	4	79	17	6.5
122	Benin	4	80	16	6.7
123	Niger	4	82	14	7.5
124	Iraq	3	74	23	5.9
125	Zimbabwe	3	56	40	6.7
126	Burkina Faso	3	71	26	6.5
127	Mali	3	70	28	8.0
128	Sierra Leone	3	74	23	6.3
129	Burundi	2	63	35	6.3
130	Togo	1	67	31	5.0

Source: Gallup World Poll 2005-2009

Wellbeing: Countries and Areas by Region

Sorted by percentage thriving

 % Thriving    **% Struggling**   **% Suffering**

Africa

RANK	COUNTRY	🡕	〰	❗	DAILY EXPERIENCE
1	Botswana	24	65	11	7.3
2	Algeria	22	71	7	6.2
3	South Africa	21	71	8	7.3
4	Tunisia	17	77	6	6.8
5	Ghana	16	79	5	7.6
6	Egypt	16	71	14	6.4
7	Nigeria	14	83	3	7.2
8	Cameroon	14	77	9	7.0
9	Malawi	14	79	7	7.5
10	Zambia	14	78	8	7.6
11	Central African Republic	12	75	13	6.4
12	Sudan	12	78	10	7.1
13	Namibia	11	79	10	8.1
14	Angola	11	81	8	6.8
15	Morocco	11	82	8	7.7
16	Mozambique	10	78	11	7.2
17	Kenya	9	78	13	7.5
18	Rwanda	8	77	15	6.9
19	Guinea	8	89	3	7.1
20	Senegal	7	87	6	7.2
21	Madagascar	7	84	10	7.0
22	Uganda	6	71	23	6.8
23	Tanzania	6	70	24	7.5
24	Ethiopia	5	65	29	7.0
25	Chad	5	88	7	7.1
26	Liberia	5	90	5	6.7
27	Congo (Kinshasa)	5	83	12	6.8

Source: Gallup World Poll 2005-2009

Wellbeing: Countries and Areas by Region
Sorted by percentage thriving

 % Thriving   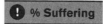 % Struggling   ❗ % Suffering

Africa (cont'd)

RANK	COUNTRY	➐	⩗	❗	DAILY EXPERIENCE
28	Mauritania	5	82	13	7.3
29	Benin	4	80	16	6.7
30	Niger	4	82	14	7.5
31	Zimbabwe	3	56	40	6.7
32	Burkina Faso	3	71	26	6.5
33	Mali	3	70	28	8.0
34	Sierra Leone	3	74	23	6.3
35	Burundi	2	63	35	6.3
36	Togo	1	67	31	5.0

Source: Gallup World Poll 2005-2009

Wellbeing: Countries and Areas by Region

Sorted by percentage thriving

 % Thriving    % Struggling   % Suffering

Asia

RANK	COUNTRY	🡕	⌁	❗	DAILY EXPERIENCE
1	New Zealand	63	35	2	7.6
2	Australia	62	35	3	7.5
3	Israel	60	36	4	6.4
4	United Arab Emirates	51	46	3	7.2
5	Saudi Arabia	48	51	1	6.8
6	Singapore	46	49	5	7.0
7	Kuwait	45	54	1	7.5
8	Cyprus	40	53	7	7.0
9	Kazakhstan	39	57	4	6.9
10	Pakistan	27	50	23	6.2
11	Malaysia	25	69	6	7.7
12	Japan	25	65	11	7.4
13	South Korea	24	61	15	6.5
14	Lebanon	23	60	17	5.8
15	Thailand	22	72	6	7.8
16	Taiwan	22	64	14	7.5
17	Azerbaijan	21	65	14	6.4
18	Uzbekistan	20	74	5	7.6
19	Iran	19	66	14	6.3
20	Tajikistan	19	74	7	6.6
21	India	19	74	7	6.5
22	Indonesia	18	72	10	8.2
23	Turkey	18	62	20	6.1
24	Vietnam	17	77	5	7.2
25	Bangladesh	16	71	13	6.9
26	Hong Kong	15	71	14	6.8
27	China	13	77	10	7.8

Source: Gallup World Poll 2005-2009

Wellbeing: Countries and Areas by Region

Sorted by percentage thriving

% Thriving | % Struggling | % Suffering

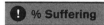

Asia (cont'd)

RANK	COUNTRY	% Thriving	% Struggling	% Suffering	DAILY EXPERIENCE
28	Philippines	13	70	18	6.7
29	Armenia	12	74	14	6.2
30	Kyrgyzstan	12	75	14	7.3
31	Palestinian Territories	11	68	21	5.5
32	Sri Lanka	10	76	15	7.1
33	Georgia	10	56	35	6.2
34	Mongolia	7	81	12	7.0
35	Nepal	7	82	11	7.4
36	Afghanistan	5	68	27	6.1
37	Cambodia	4	79	17	6.5
38	Iraq	3	74	23	5.9

Source: Gallup World Poll 2005-2009

Wellbeing: Countries and Areas by Region

Sorted by percentage thriving

 % Thriving    % Struggling   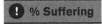 % Suffering

Americas

RANK	COUNTRY			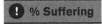	DAILY EXPERIENCE
1	Canada	68	31	1	7.8
2	Mexico	52	44	4	7.8
3	Panama	51	46	2	8.2
4	United States	50	47	4	7.6
5	Puerto Rico	47	45	8	7.6
6	Jamaica	46	49	5	7.7
7	Trinidad and Tobago	44	51	5	7.9
8	Colombia	44	48	7	7.4
9	Belize	44	50	6	6.8
10	Venezuela	42	52	6	8.0
11	Costa Rica	40	54	6	7.9
12	Brazil	37	57	6	7.4
13	Argentina	33	58	8	7.2
14	Guatemala	33	59	8	7.8
15	Chile	32	56	12	7.0
16	Guyana	31	64	5	7.0
17	Uruguay	31	58	11	7.3
18	Dominican Republic	28	53	19	6.8
19	Honduras	26	59	14	7.7
20	Cuba	24	66	11	6.7
21	Peru	23	56	20	6.9
22	Ecuador	22	62	15	7.6
23	Nicaragua	21	56	23	7.4
24	Bolivia	21	69	10	6.9
25	El Salvador	16	56	28	7.8
26	Haiti	4	60	35	6.2

Source: Gallup World Poll 2005-2009

Wellbeing: Countries and Areas by Region

Sorted by percentage thriving

 % Thriving  **% Struggling** 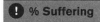 **% Suffering**

Europe

RANK	COUNTRY	⬀	⩗	❗	DAILY EXPERIENCE
1	Denmark	82	17	1	7.9
2	Finland	75	23	2	7.8
3	Ireland	72	28	0	8.1
4	Norway	69	31	0	7.9
5	Sweden	68	30	2	7.9
6	Netherlands	68	32	1	7.7
7	Switzerland	62	36	2	7.6
8	Spain	60	37	3	7.3
9	Austria	57	40	3	7.7
10	United Kingdom	56	41	3	7.4
11	Belgium	56	41	3	7.3
12	France	49	49	2	7.0
13	Greece	44	49	7	7.1
14	Italy	42	52	6	6.7
15	Czech Republic	39	51	9	6.6
16	Germany	36	56	7	7.3
17	Russia	31	56	13	7.1
18	Lithuania	29	55	16	6.1
19	Kosovo	29	65	6	6.2
20	Poland	28	61	10	7.1
21	Slovenia	28	58	13	7.0
22	Belarus	26	63	11	7.0
23	Portugal	22	61	17	7.1
24	Romania	21	56	23	6.6
25	Slovakia	21	60	19	6.5
26	Estonia	20	64	16	7.0

Source: Gallup World Poll 2005-2009

Wellbeing: Countries and Areas by Region
Sorted by percentage thriving

Europe (cont'd)

RANK	COUNTRY	 % Thriving	% Struggling	% Suffering	DAILY EXPERIENCE
27	Ukraine	20	58	22	6.7
28	Latvia	18	62	20	7.0
29	Hungary	13	53	34	6.9
30	Bulgaria	6	58	36	6.5

Source: Gallup World Poll 2005-2009

Global Wellbeing Study: Methodology

The world tables show life evaluation estimates of the percentage "thriving," "struggling," and "suffering" for countries and regions across the world. Percentages were derived based on responses to the Cantril Self-Anchoring Striving Scale. The tables also provide daily wellbeing averages (0-10 scoring) based on responses to 10 items measuring daily experiences (feeling well-rested, being treated with respect, smiling/laughter, learning/interest, enjoyment, physical pain, worry, sadness, stress, and anger). Each daily experience is scored dichotomously with higher scores representing better days (more positive and less negative daily experience or affect).

As part of Gallup's ongoing global research, we continually survey residents in more than 150 countries, representing more than 98% of the world's adult population, using randomly selected, nationally representative samples. Gallup typically surveys 1,000 individuals in each country using a standard set of core questions that has been translated into the major languages of the respective country. In some regions, supplemental questions are asked in addition to core questions. Face-to-face interviews last approximately one hour, while telephone interviews are about 30 minutes. In many countries, the survey is conducted once per year, and fieldwork is generally completed in two to four weeks. Data from the United States were gathered via the Gallup-Healthways Well-Being Index (January 2-December 30, 2009), including surveys of 350,000 individuals.

Gallup is entirely responsible for the management, design, and control of this global research study. For the past 70 years, Gallup has been committed to the principle that accurately collecting and disseminating the opinions and aspirations of people around the world is vital to understanding our world. Gallup's mission is to provide information in an objective, reliable, and scientifically grounded manner.

The maximum margin of error is calculated around reported proportions for each country-level data set, assuming a 95% confidence level. The margin of error also includes the approximate design effect for the total country sample. For reported percentages based on the total country data set (not subset), the margin of error is ±3.7 percentage points. This means that if the survey was conducted 100 times using the exact same procedures, the "true value" around a reported percentage of 50 would fall within the range of 46.3% to 53.7% in 95 out of 100 cases.

Other factors that can affect survey validity include measurement error associated with the questionnaire such as translation issues, and coverage error, where a part of the target population has a zero probability of being selected for the survey. Additionally, because of authoritarian governments in select countries, respondents may be less than forthcoming in their assessments, leading to the potential for inflated scores.

References

This book covers a wide range of research. For more detail about Gallup's research and other studies referenced in the book's text, please see this expanded reference section.

References are listed by section and order of occurrence. The page number and the text corresponding to each reference is copied from the book's narrative. For select references, we have included additional commentary.

Introductory Section: Your Wellbeing

4   *Gallup scientists have been exploring the demands of a life well-lived since the mid-20th century:* Gallup, G., & Hill, E. (1960). *The secrets of a long life.* New York: Bernard Geis.

5   *We then compared these results to how people experience their days and evaluate their lives overall:* In *each* of these countries, Gallup interviewed more than 1,000 randomly selected citizens (more than 150,000 in total). The topics of the questions ranged from basic needs of food, water, and shelter to much higher level needs such as having a job that fits one's strengths and being engaged in the community. To allow for global comparison, we used a common set of questions and methodologies across these countries.

5   *To create this assessment, the Wellbeing Finder, we tested hundreds of questions across countries, languages, and vastly different life situations:* Farmers; city dwellers; full-time workers; retirees; students; people in good and poor health; people of all income levels; people who were married, divorced, and widowed.

6   *Career Wellbeing:* Career Wellbeing is about the occupation or vocation you do for a living and was tested to ensure that it extends beyond traditional job settings to students, those who are retired, stay-at-home parents, and others. For more information on how each of these elements was tested to ensure their applicability across different groups, see Appendix D: Technical Report: The Research and Development of Gallup's Wellbeing Metrics.

6   *Social Wellbeing:* To test this construct rigorously, we included sufficient numbers of people who were married, separated, divorced, widowed, never married, or living with a partner.

6   *Financial Wellbeing:* We tested questions within this category across various income groups to make sure they were appropriate for people with below-average, middle, and high incomes.

6   *Physical Wellbeing:* To find questions that would be applicable to people in different physical situations around the world, we studied the young, the old, the healthy, and the unhealthy.

6   *Community Wellbeing:* We studied people who lived in cities, suburbs, and rural areas to make sure the questions would apply to someone living in the middle of an urban center or on a remote farm.

8-9   *But the reality is, our short-term self still wins and gets dessert, despite objections from our long-term self that wants a healthy body and a long life:* Schelling, T.C. (1978). Egonomics, or the art of self-management. *The American Economic Review, 68*(2), 290-294.

9   *But when we asked the same group of people later in the survey if there was a bowl of candy sitting right in front of them if they would eat some, more than 70% admitted they would:* For this Gallup Panel study, we interviewed 23,449 people in August 2009.

9   *Or we might choose to exercise tomorrow morning because we know that just 20 minutes of activity can boost our mood for the next 12 hours:* Sibold, J.S., & Berg, K. (2009, May 29). *Mood enhancement persists for up to 12 hours following aerobic exercise.* Poster session presented at the annual meeting of the American College of Sports Medicine, Seattle, WA.

10   *In the sections that follow, we refer to people we interviewed who have thriving wellbeing in each of the five elements:* Refer to the book's appendices to learn more about how "thriving" is defined. To protect the confidentiality of people we interviewed, their real names are not used.

1: Career Wellbeing

15   *Yet only 20% of people can give a strong "yes" in response:* For this Gallup Panel study, we interviewed 2,307 people. (Internationally, we interviewed 10,598 people, and 19% of those respondents strongly agreed with the "Do you like what you do each day?" question.)

16   *People with high Career Wellbeing are more than* twice *as likely to be thriving in their lives overall:* For this Gallup Panel study, we interviewed 14,366 people and controlled for gender, age, income, and education.

16-17   *This study followed 130,000 people for several decades, allowing researchers to look at the way major life events such as marriage, divorce, birth of a child, or death of a spouse affect our life satisfaction over time:* Clark, A.E., Diener, E., Georgellis, Y., & Lucas, R.E. (2008). Lags and leads in life satisfaction: A test of the baseline hypothesis. *The Economic Journal, 118*(529), F222-F243. The chart adapted from this article merges data for males and females; however, as noted, the long-term impact of sustained unemployment is much stronger for men than for women.

19   *As part of the experiment, the participants carried a handheld device that alerted them at various points in the day when we would ask them what they were doing, who they were with, and several other questions about their mood:* Stone, A., & Harter, J.K. (2009). *The experience of work: A momentary perspective.* Omaha, NE: Gallup.

21   *So if your Career Wellbeing is thriving, you are able to have good* weekends *and good weekdays, and the time you are at work is as enjoyable as the time you spend away from work:* Our field sites were located at Stony Brook University and Syracuse University, supervised by Arthur Stone, Ph.D.; Leighann Litcher-Kelly, Ph.D.; and Joshua Smyth, Ph.D. Salivary assays were collected randomly six times per day (twice each during the morning, afternoon, and evening) on Thursday, Friday, and

Saturday. Momentary cortisol followed the typical diurnal cycle, with higher cortisol in the mornings. After controlling for time of day, momentary cortisol was significantly associated with momentary stress, happiness, and interest. Moments with higher stress and lower happiness and interest corresponded with higher cortisol. Employee engagement was measured with the Gallup Q[12]. Cortisol was significantly higher on the weekday mornings for workers with lower engagement, in comparison to those with high engagement. There were no differences in morning cortisol between more highly and less highly engaged workers on Saturdays.

22   *The extreme variation between a good weekend and a bad weekday might explain why heart attacks are more likely to occur on Mondays:* Witte, D.R., Grobbee, D.E., Bots, M.L., & Hoes, A.W. (2005). A meta-analysis of excess cardiac mortality on Monday. *European Journal of Epidemiology, 20*(5), 401-406.

The following table summarizes Gallup and Healthways' daily tracking of wellbeing across the United States. For most people, weekends and holidays are much better than weekdays.

Differences in Daily Mood in the U.S.

TYPE OF DAY	PERCENTAGE WITH A LOT OF HAPPINESS/ ENJOYMENT WITHOUT A LOT OF STRESS/ WORRY	PERCENTAGE WITH A LOT OF STRESS/ WORRY WITHOUT A LOT OF HAPPINESS/ ENJOYMENT	RATIO OF HAPPINESS TO STRESS
Weekdays (Not Holidays)	44%	12%	4:1
Weekends and Holidays	56%	9%	6:1

Source: Gallup-Healthways Well-Being Index

23   *So when we transition from a leisurely Sunday, the least stressful day of the week, to Monday morning in a workplace where we are not engaged, it might damage our bodies in the process:* In addition to posing the potential risk of heart attacks on Mondays, sustained high levels of cortisol can do even more damage over time. Elevated cortisol can raise blood pressure, weaken the immune system, slow healing, suppress thyroid function, create blood sugar imbalances, decrease bone density, and impair thinking. High stress levels throughout the workweek may lead to a host of physical problems, especially for those who are disengaged in their jobs. In contrast, for those who are engaged in their jobs, engagement provides a buffer against negative emotions and major spikes in stress levels.

Steptoe, A., Wardle, J., & Marmot, M. (2005). Positive affect and health-related neuroendocrine, cardiovascular, and inflammatory processes. *PNAS, 102*(18), 6508-6512.

Schlotz, W., Hellhammer, J., Schulz, P., & Stone, A.A. (2004). Perceived work overload and chronic worrying predict weekend-weekday differences in cortisol awakening response. *Psychosomatic Medicine, 66*(2), 207-214.

Ebrecht, M., Hextall, J., Kirtley, L.G., Taylor, A., Dyson, M., & Weinman, J. (2004). Perceived stress and cortisol levels predict speed of wound healing in healthy adult males. *Psychoneuroendocrinology, 29*(6), 798-809.

23   *Boosting Career Wellbeing might also reduce the risk of anxiety and depression:* Agrawal, S., & Harter, J.K. (2009). Engagement at work predicts change in depression and anxiety status in the next year. Omaha, NE: Gallup.

24   *When we contacted the remaining panel members in 2009, we again asked them if they had been diagnosed with depression in the last year:* For this Gallup Panel study, we interviewed 9,561 people.

24   *Further, those who were actively disengaged in their careers in 2008 were nearly* **twice as likely to be diagnosed with depression** *over the next year:* For this longitudinal study of full-time and part-time workers, we interviewed 7,993 people with no history of diagnosed depression and tracked their disease burden from 2008 to 2009. As of March 2009, 483 new cases of diagnosed depression were recorded. We then studied how employee engagement in 2008 predicted changes in depression status (new diagnosis) in 2009.

Odds of Being Diagnosed With Depression Over the Next Year

Engaged in Career	4.6%
Not Engaged in Career	6.0%
Actively Disengaged in Career	8.8%

24   *In another study, we tracked employees for two years to examine the relationship between changes in engagement at work and changes in cholesterol and triglyceride levels:* Harter, J.K., Canedy, J., & Stone, A. (2008). *A longitudinal study of engagement at work and physiologic indicators of health.* Presented at the 2008 Work, Stress, and Health Conference, Washington, D.C. For this study, we tracked 331 employees over a two-year time period.

24-25   *As employees' levels of engagement at work increased, their total cholesterol and triglyceride levels significantly decreased. And those with decreasing levels of engagement at work had an increase in total cholesterol and triglycerides:* These patterns were even more evident for workers who were 55 or older, and the findings held true after statistically controlling for health history, medication use, gender, and a variety of other variables.

25   *Time-use studies provide important data about what people do with their time, who they spend it with, and how they feel at various points throughout the day:* For more detail on this topic, see Appendix B: Daily Wellbeing: How We Spend Our Time.

Kahneman, D., Krueger, A.B., Schkade, D., Schwarz, N., & Stone, A. (2004). Toward national well-being accounts. *The American Economic Review, 94*(2), 429-434.

Kahneman, D., Krueger, A.B., Schkade, D.A., Schwarz, N., & Stone, A.A. (2004). A survey method for characterizing daily life experience: The day reconstruction method. *Science, 306*, 1776-1780.

25   *One of the major findings from this research is that the person we* **least** *enjoy being around is our boss:* Krueger, A.B., Kahneman, D., Schkade, D., Schwarz, N., & Stone, A.A. (2008). *National time accounting: The currency of life (Working Papers No. 1061).* Princeton, NJ: Princeton University, Department of Economics, Industrial Relations Section.

25   *This helps explain why a study of more than 3,000 workers in Sweden found that those who deemed their managers to be the least competent had a 24% higher risk of a serious heart problem:* Nyberg, A., Alfredsson, L., Theorell, T., Westerlund,

H., Vahtera, J., & Kivimaki, M. (2009). Managerial leadership and ischaemic heart disease among employees: The Swedish WOLF study. *Occupational and Environmental Medicine*, *66*(1), 51-55.

26   *But if your manager is primarily focusing on your strengths, the chance of your being actively disengaged is just 1%, or 1 in 100:* Rath, T. (2007). *StrengthsFinder 2.0*. New York: Gallup Press.

27   *According to one study, by the time people reach their 50s, nearly two-thirds* want *to keep working:* MetLife Foundation/Civic Ventures. (2005, June). *New Face of Work Survey*. Retrieved September 1, 2009, from http://www.civicventures.org/publications/surveys/new_face_of_work/new_face_of_work.pdf

27   *Even more remarkable, 93% of these men reported getting a great deal of satisfaction out of the work they did, and 86% reported having* fun *doing their job:* Public Opinion Surveys, Inc. (1959). *Who lives to be 95 and older?: A study of 402 Americans 95 years of age and over*. Princeton, NJ.

27-28   *When we build on our strengths and daily successes — instead of focusing on failures — we simply learn more:* Dye, D. (2009, August 26). *We learn more from success, not failure*. Retrieved December 18, 2009, from ABC News Web site: http://abcnews.go.com/Technology/DyeHard/story?id=8319006

28   *Compared to those who do* not *get to focus on what they do best, people who have the opportunity to use their strengths are* six times *as likely to be engaged in their jobs and more than* three times *as likely to report having an excellent quality of life:* Rath, T. (2007). *StrengthsFinder 2.0*. New York: Gallup Press.

28   *Our global data show that these people can enjoy a full 40-hour workweek, while those who* do not *get to use their strengths get burned out after just 20 hours of work per week:* When we surveyed random samples of people from around the world, we asked them how many hours they worked the day before. We also asked them various questions about their experiences and emotions throughout that day. For those who had low Career Wellbeing and who *did not* have a chance to use their strengths, their energy started to deteriorate rapidly after just four hours a day, or the equivalent of a 20-hour workweek.

When we studied those who had higher Career Wellbeing and who *did* have a chance to use their strengths regularly, this group was able to work for at least eight hours a day (a 40-hour workweek equivalent) and in some cases, up to 13 hours a day, without experiencing a similar decline. When compared to the raw number of hours worked, Career Wellbeing had *three times* the impact on the way people view their overall quality of life.

Harter, J.K., & Arora, R. (2009). The impact of time spent working and job fit on well-being around the world. In E. Diener, D. Kahneman, & J. Helliwell. (Eds.), *International Differences in Well-Being* (pp. 389-426). Oxford, UK: Oxford University Press.

28   *By no means are you immune from getting exhausted and stressed out — even if you have a job you love:* We can see this in the data, even for people with high Career Wellbeing. The only emotion we studied that actually continued to improve beyond eight hours worked — for those with high Career Wellbeing — was pride.

2: Social Wellbeing

33 *Because we tend to synchronize our moods with the people around us, our emotions influence one another throughout the day:* Ekman, P. (2003). *Emotions revealed: Recognizing faces and feelings to improve communication and emotional life.* New York: Henry Holt and Company, LLC.

34 *This research, which was based on a 30+ year longitudinal study of more than 12,000 people who were all part of one interconnected network, found that your odds of being happy increase by 15% if a direct connection in your social network is happy:* Fowler, J.H., & Christakis, N.A. (2008). Dynamic spread of happiness in a large social network: Longitudinal analysis over 20 years in the Framingham heart study. *BMJ, 337,* a2338+.

35 *According to this research, an increase of about $10,000 in annual income was associated with just a 2% increased likelihood of being happy:* Christakis, N.A., & Fowler, J.H. (2009). *Connected: The surprising power of our social networks and how they shape our lives.* New York: Little, Brown and Company.

35 *As Harvard researcher Nicholas Christakis summarized: "People are embedded in social networks and the health and wellbeing of one person affects the health and wellbeing of others. . . . Human happiness is not merely the province of isolated individuals":* Fowler, J.H., & Christakis, N.A. (2008). Dynamic spread of happiness in a large social network: Longitudinal analysis over 20 years in the Framingham heart study. *BMJ, 337,* a2338+.

35   *In this context, it's easy to see how peer pressure has cut smoking rates in half over the last few decades:* Christakis, N.A., & Fowler, J.H. (2009). *Connected: The surprising power of our social networks and how they shape our lives.* New York: Little, Brown and Company.

35   *Over the span of this study, smokers were essentially pushed out to the edges of the network between 1971 and 2000:* Christakis, N.A., & Fowler, J.H. (2008). The collective dynamics of smoking in a large social network. *New England Journal of Medicine, 358*(21), 2249-2258.

36   *And if your spouse becomes obese, the odds of your becoming obese go up by 37%:* Christakis, N.A., & Fowler, J.H. (2007). The spread of obesity in a large social network over 32 years. *The New England Journal of Medicine, 357*(4), 370-379.

36   *We found that people with a best friend who has a very healthy diet are more than* five times as likely *to have a very healthy diet as well:* Rath, T. (2006). *Vital friends: The people you can't afford to live without.* New York: Gallup Press.

37   *Relationships serve as a buffer during tough times, which in turn improves our cardiovascular functioning and decreases stress levels:* DukeMed News. (2004, April 13). *Isolated heart patients have twice the risk of dying, present challenges to health care workers.* Retrieved August 19, 2005, from http://www. emaxhealth.com/39/176.html

37-38   *On the other hand, people with very few social ties have nearly twice the risk of dying from heart disease and are twice as likely to catch colds — even though they are less likely to have the exposure to germs that comes from frequent social contact:* Rath, T. (2006). *Vital friends: The people you can't afford to live without.* New York: Gallup Press.

Cohen, S., Doyle, W.J., Turner, R., Alper, C.M., & Skoner, D.P. (2003). Sociability and susceptibility to the common cold. *Psychological Science, 14*(5), 389-395.

38   *To study how one of our closest relationships influences our physical health, a team of researchers designed a clever experiment in which they studied how stress levels affect the time it takes to recover from a wound:* Kiecolt-Glaser, J.K., Loving, T.J., Stowell, J.R., Malarkey, W.B., Lemeshow, S., Dickinson, S.L., et al. (2005). Hostile marital interactions, proinflammatory cytokine production, and wound healing. *Archives of General Psychiatry, 62*(12), 1377-1384.

38   *As scientists continue to explore the connection between our relationships and our health, they are discovering that our Social Wellbeing might have* **even more influence on how quickly we recover** *than conventional risk factors:* Boden-Albala, B., Litwak, E., Elkind, M.S.V., & Sacco, R.L. (2005). Social isolation and outcomes post stroke. *Neurology, 64*(11), 1888-1892.

39   *The data suggest that to have a thriving day, we need* **six hours** *of social time:* We tracked the daily emotions of more than 140,000 Americans with the Gallup-Healthways Well-Being Index. As part of this ongoing study, we ask people to tell us

whether they had a lot of enjoyment, happiness, worry, and stress the previous day. We also record the number of hours they recall spending with friends and family the previous day (including time on the phone, electronic messaging, etc.). We compared number of hours of social time to daily mood.

Harter, J.K., & Arora, R. (2008, June 5). *Social time crucial to daily emotional well-being in U.S.* Retrieved September 23, 2009, from Gallup Web site: http://www.gallup.com/poll/107692/ Social-Time-Crucial-Daily-Emotional-WellBeing.aspx

As you can see from the following table, each hour of social time continues to improve the odds of having a good day, up to about six hours.

Hours of Social Time and Daily Mood

HOURS OF SOCIAL TIME IN A DAY	PERCENTAGE WITH A LOT OF HAPPINESS/ ENJOYMENT WITHOUT A LOT OF STRESS/WORRY	PERCENTAGE WITH A LOT OF STRESS/WORRY WITHOUT A LOT OF HAPPINESS/ ENJOYMENT	RATIO OF HAPPINESS TO STRESS
0	32%	27%	1:1
0.1 to 1	35%	20%	2:1
1.1 to 2	40%	15%	3:1
2.1 to 3	44%	11%	4:1
3.1 to 4	49%	8%	6:1
4.1 to 5	51%	7%	7:1
5.1 to 6	54%	6%	9:1
6.1 to 7	54%	5%	11:1
7.1 to 8	56%	6%	9:1
8.1 to 9	56%	6%	9:1
More than 9	56%	6%	9:1

Source: Gallup-Healthways Well-Being Index

40   *A study of more than 15,000 people over the age of 50 found that among those who were socially active, their memories declined at less than half the rate compared to those who were the least social:* Ertel, K.A., Glymour, M.M., Berkman, L.F. (2008). Effects of social integration on preserving memory function in a nationally representative US elderly population. *American Public Health Association, 98*(7), 1215-1220.

41   *The researchers found that even small increases in social cohesiveness lead to large gains in production:* Economist.com. (2008, August 20). Technology Monitor. *Every move you make.* Retrieved September 22, 2009, from www.economist.com/ science/tm/displaystory.cfm?story_id=11957553

42   *One study revealed that marital strain actually accelerates the decline in our physical health as we age:* Umberson, D., Williams, K., Powers, D.A., Liu, H., Needham, B. (2006). You make me sick: Marital quality and health over the life course. *Journal of Health and Social Behavior, 47*(1), 1-16.

      This was an eight-year study of more than 1,000 married individuals.

42   *Our research has found that people who have at least three or four very close friendships are healthier, have higher wellbeing, and are more engaged in their jobs:* Rath, T. (2006). *Vital friends: The people you can't afford to live without.* New York: Gallup Press.

42-43   *The Harvard research on social networks revealed that, while*
         each happy friend increases your odds of being happy by about
         9%, each unhappy friend only decreases your odds of being happy
         by 7%: Christakis, N.A., & Fowler, J.H. (2009). *Connected: The*
         surprising power of our social networks and how they shape our
         lives. New York: Little, Brown and Company.

3: Financial Wellbeing

50   *Clearly, wealthier countries have citizens with higher wellbeing:*
         Deaton, A. (2008). Income, health, and well-being around
         the world: Evidence from the Gallup World Poll. *Journal of*
         Economic Perspectives, 22, 2.

The Economics of Wellbeing figure plots the relationship
between per capita GDP and mean scores across respondents
for each country based on the Cantril Self-Anchoring Striving
Scale, which asks respondents to imagine a ladder with steps
numbered from 0 at the bottom to 10 at the top, with 0
representing the worst possible life and 10 representing the
best possible life, and to assess on which step of the ladder they
would say they personally feel they stand at the present time.
After converting per-capita GDP to *logarithm* per-capita GDP,
the correlation between wellbeing (life evaluation on the Cantril
Scale) and income is .84, indicating that every doubling of
income adds a full point (0-10 scale) to one's overall wellbeing.
A further analysis by Stevenson and Wolfers confirmed these
findings and "found no evidence of a satiation point beyond
which wealthier countries have no further increases in subjective
well-being." They also found linear relationships between income
and wellbeing for individuals in most countries and positive
relationships between economic growth and wellbeing. From

this, one can infer that higher income improves the odds of high wellbeing. Further research distinguishes between different types of wellbeing measures and their differential relationships with income. The findings indicate daily experiences and affect are less highly correlated with income than are judgments of overall life (life evaluation). Therefore, income is more highly related to life evaluation than it is to daily experiences or feelings.

Stevenson, B., & Wolfers, J. (2008 September). *Economic growth and subjective well-being: Reassessing the Easterlin paradox.* CESifo Working Paper No. 2394, CESifo Group.

Diener, E., Kahneman, D., Arora, R., Harter, J., & Tov, W. (2009). Income's differential influence on judgments of life versus affective well-being. In A.C. Michalos (Ed.), *Social indicators research series: vol. 39. Assessing well-being: The collected works of Ed Diener* (pp. 233-246). London, UK: Springer.

52   *For example, across Africa, 56% of people we studied reported that there were times when their family had "gone hungry" in the last 12 months:* Across the Americas, that number is 16%. In Asia, 9% report that someone in their family has gone hungry, and in Europe, just 3% say they or their family have been without food.

53   *When a team of Harvard researchers surveyed people about their spending on themselves, their spending on others, and their happiness, they found that spending on oneself does* not *boost wellbeing. However, spending money on others does — and it appears to be as important to people's happiness as the total amount of money they make:* Dunn, E.W., Aknin, L.B., & Norton, M.I. (2008). Spending money on others promotes happiness. *Science, 319*(5870), 1687-1688.

54   *Sadness may even lead us to spend* a lot more *money on ourselves than we otherwise would:* Sadness may encourage more extravagance. (2008, February 8). *The New York Times.* Retrieved September 4, 2009, from http://www.nytimes.com

55   *Even if you feel better immediately after your purchase, studies show that our satisfaction with material goods decreases over time:* Carter, T.J., & Gilovich, T. (2010). The relative relativity of material and experiential purchases. *Journal of Personality and Social Psychology, 98*(1), 146-159.

55   *Even brief experiential purchases such as dining out or going to a movie increase our wellbeing:* Van Boven, L., & Gilovich, T. (2003). To do or to have? That is the question. *Journal of Personality and Social Psychology, 85*(6), 1193-1202.

55   *In addition to satisfying our need for social time, we are less likely to regret experiential purchases, which increases our satisfaction with these decisions over time:* Carter, T.J., & Gilovich, T. (2010). The relative relativity of material and experiential purchases. *Journal of Personality and Social Psychology, 98*(1), 146-159.

56   *For those who make less than $25,000 a year, experiential and material purchases produce similar gains in wellbeing:* Van Boven, L., & Gilovich, T. (2003). To do or to have? That is the question. *Journal of Personality and Social Psychology, 85*(6), 1193-1202.

57   *Instead, nearly half the people presented with these options pick the lower salary of $50,000 a year:* Solnick, S.J., & Hemenway, D. (1998). Is more always better?: A survey on positional concerns. *Journal of Economic Behavior & Organization, 37*(3), 373-383.

59   *In other words, it hurts a lot more to lose $50 that we already have than it feels good to win $50:* Thaler, R.H. (1999). Mental accounting matters. *Journal of Behavioral Decision Making,* *12*(3), 183-206.

60   *As University of Chicago economist Richard Thaler describes, credit cards act as a "decoupling device" because they separate the joy of the immediate purchase from the pain of the payment, which is off in the distant future:* Thaler, R.H. (1999). Mental accounting matters. *Journal of Behavioral Decision Making,* *12*(3), 183-206.

61   *Research has shown that when a company requires employees to explicitly opt in to a retirement plan, most workers do not participate. But when the default is for employees to be automatically enrolled,* **more than 80% participate** *in the retirement plan:* Nessmith, W.E., Utkus, S.P., & Young, J.A. (2007, December). *Measuring the effectiveness of automatic enrollment.* Retrieved September 22, 2009, from the Vanguard Center for Retirement Research Web site: https:// institutional.vanguard.com/VGApp/iip/site/institutional/ researchcommentary/article?File=EffectivenessAutoEnrollment

Companies are rapidly moving toward plans that feature automatic enrollment to help their employees build a stable financial future. In 2003, only 8% of 401(k) plans offered automatic enrollment. By 2007, this number had risen to 36% for all companies and more than 51% for large companies (with 5,000 or more eligible employees offered automatic enrollment).

Automatic Enrollment in Retirement Plan Participation

	ALL WORKERS	INCOME LESS THAN $30,000
Without Automatic Enrollment	45%	25%
With Automatic Enrollment	86%	77%

Adapted from Nessmith, et al., *Measuring the Effectiveness of Automatic Enrollment*, December 2007.

Orszag, P. (2008, August 7). *Behavioral economics: Lessons from retirement research for health care and beyond*. Presentation at the Retirement Research Consortium. Retrieved September 22, 2009, from http://www.cbo.gov/ftpdocs/96xx/doc9673/Presentation_RRC.1.1.shtml

62 *So after reviewing the income levels of the people we interviewed, we conducted a deeper analysis of the key drivers of Financial Wellbeing:* As part of the research we conducted while creating the Wellbeing Finder, we asked a host of questions about each person's Financial Wellbeing, including annual income. From previous research collected as part of our World Poll, we knew that income played an important, but incomplete, role in wellbeing. So we designed a study to pit money against worry and financial security. We conducted a regression analysis to explore the relative importance of annual income, worry about money, and financial security. Regression analysis allows researchers to study the independent contribution of each variable while controlling — or statistically adjusting — for other variables, such as education, age, gender, or marital status.

4: Physical Wellbeing

71   *New research suggests that a single meal high in saturated fat reduces our arteries' ability to carry enough blood to our bodies and brains:* Murray, A.J., Knight, N.S., Cochlin, L.E., McAleese, S., Deacon, R.M.J., Rawlins, N.P., et al. (2009). Deterioration of physical performance and cognitive function in rats with short-term high-fat feeding [Electronic version]. *The FASEB Journal, 23*, 1-8.

71-72   *According to NYU's Gerald Weissmann, M.D., this "high-fat hangover" could also slow us down and impair our thinking:* 'High-fat hangover': Eating fatty foods lowers memory function in brains, bodies. (2009, August 14). *Daily News*. Retrieved December 19, 2009, from http://www.nydailynews.com

Murray, A.J., Knight, N.S., Cochlin, L.E., McAleese, S., Deacon, R.M.J., Rawlins, J.N.P., et al. (2009). Deterioration of physical performance and cognitive function in rats with short-term high-fat feeding [Electronic version]. *The FASEB Journal, 23*, 1-8.

Nicholls, S.J., Lundman, P., Harmer, J.A., Cutri, B., Griffiths, K.A., Rye, K., et al. (2006). Consumption of saturated fat impairs the anti-inflammatory properties of high-density lipoproteins and endothelial function. *Journal of the American College of Cardiology, 48*(4), 715-720.

Winocur, G., & Greenwood, C.E. (2005). Studies of the effects of high fat diets on cognitive function in a rat model. *Neurobiology of Aging, 26*(1), 46-49.

72   *Simply knowing that eating fried foods puts us at a 30% greater risk for a heart attack down the road doesn't change our short-term decisions:* Iqbal, R., Anand, S., Ounpuu, S., Islam, S., Zhang, X., Rangarajan, S., et al. (2008). Dietary patterns and the risk of acute myocardial infarction in 52 countries: Results of the INTERHEART study. *Circulation, 118*(19), 1929-1937.

74   *One study found that men who have a specific gene that predisposes them to prostate cancer were able to suppress the expression of this gene substantially by eating the equivalent of just one portion of broccoli per week:* The results of this study suggest that even a few portions of cruciferous vegetables (e.g., broccoli or cauliflower) per week can have significant effects on gene expression by changing cell signaling pathways. Information is transferred through these signaling pathways that can increase the signal to the cell's nucleus where gene expression occurs.

Traka, M., Gasper, A.V., Melchini, A., Bacon, J.R., Needs, P.W., Frost, V., et al. (2008). Broccoli consumption interacts with GSTM1 to perturb oncogenic signalling pathways in the prostate [Electronic version]. *PLoS ONE, 3*(7), e2568, 1-14.

74   *This newly discovered phenomenon, known as "epigenetic inheritance," is much more common than we think:* Jablonka, E., & Raz, G. (2009). Transgenerational epigenetic inheritance: Prevalence, mechanisms, and implications for the study of heredity and evolution. *The Quarterly Review of Biology, 84*(2), 131-176.

75   *For example, a study of 60,000 women revealed that eating*
        one or more servings of fatty fish (e.g., salmon) per week could
        reduce the risk of kidney cancer by 74%: Wolk, A., Larsson,
        S.C., Johansson, J., & Ekman, P. (2006). Long-term fatty fish
        consumption and renal cell carcinoma incidence in women.
        Journal of the American Medical Association, 296(11), 1371-1376.

75   *Higher levels of omega-3 fatty acids have been shown to*
        be protective against a wide range of cancers, cognitive
        degeneration such as Alzheimer's, heart disease, and a wide
        range of other conditions: El-Mesery, M.E., Al-Gayyar, M.M.,
        Salem, H.A., Darweish, M.D., & El-Mowafy, A.M. (2009
        April 2). Chemopreventive and renal protective effect for
        docosahexaenoic acid (DHA): Implications of CRP and lipid
        peroxides. *Cell Division, 4*(6). Retrieved December 20, 2009,
        from http://www.celldiv.com/content/pdf/1747-1028-4-6.pdf

        Freund-Levi, Y., Eriksdotter-Jonhagen, M., Cederholm, T.,
        Basun, H., Faxen-Irving, G., Garlind, A., et al. (2006). ω-3
        fatty acid treatment in 174 patients with mild to moderate
        Alzheimer disease: OmegAD study. *Archives of Neurology, 63*,
        1402-1408.

        Mayo Clinic. (2007). The power of 3. *Mayo Clinic Health Letter*,
        25(8), 6.

75   *Other studies have revealed how high levels of omega-3s*
        moderate symptoms of depression, decrease impulsiveness, and
        boost our daily mood: Conklin, S.M., Manuck, S.B., Yao, J.K.,
        Flory, J.D., Hibbeln, J.R., & Muldoon, M.F. (2007). High
        omega-6 and low omega-3 fatty acids are associated with
        depressive symptoms and neuroticism. *Psychosomatic Medicine*,
        69(9), 932-934.

75   *A 2009 experiment that explored the consumption ratio of omega-6 fatty acids to omega-3s might explain why the consumption of omega-3s also decreases inflammation (pain), asthma, diabetes, and arthritis:* Weaver, K.L., Ivester, P., Seeds, M., Case, L.D., Arm, J.P., & Chilton, F.H. (2009). Effect of dietary fatty acids on inflammatory gene expression in healthy humans. *The Journal of Biological Chemistry, 284*(23), 15400-15407.

Based on the latest research, a combination of a low-fat, low-carbohydrate diet with minimal meat consumption might be the best route to long-term health. While it is possible to lose weight on a low-carbohydrate/higher fat diet that includes lots of red meat, this can come at the cost of raising LDL or "bad cholesterol." Recent studies have shown that meat derived from animal muscle typically contains large amounts of saturated fat and cholesterol, thus making it the likely culprit in boosting the bad cholesterol levels.

Jenkins, D.J.A., Wong, J.M.W., Kendall, C.W.C, Esfahani, A., Ng, V.W.Y., Leong, T.C.K., et al. (2009). The effect of a plant-based low-carbohydrate ("Eco-Atkins") diet on body weight and blood lipid concentrations in hyperlipidemic subjects. *Archives of Internal Medicine, 169*(11), 1046-1054.

76   *They discovered that many critical signaling genes that promote inflammation, autoimmune, and allergic responses were markedly reduced in* just five weeks *due to these dietary changes:* What we eat might even make us smarter and reduce the risk of cancer. A study of more than 5,000 Canadian students revealed that students who had higher fruit and vegetable intake (and less caloric intake from fat) were 41% less likely

to fail a basic literacy assessment, even when the researchers controlled for socioeconomic disadvantages.

Florence, M.D., Asbridge, M., & Veugelers, P.J. (2008). Diet quality and academic performance. *Journal of School Health*, *78*(4), 209-215.

Ma, R.W-L., & Chapman, K. (2009). A systematic review of the effect of diet in prostate cancer prevention and treatment. *Journal of Human Nutrition and Dietetics*, *22*(3), 187-199.

76   *Instead, the foods we eat might be tricking our body into thinking it needs more fat, thus starting a vicious cycle:* Kirchner, H., Gutierrez, J.A., Solenberg, P.J., Pfluger, P.T., Czyzyk, T.A., Willency, J.A., et al. (2009). GOAT links dietary lipids with the endocrine control of energy balance. *Nature Medicine*, *15*(7), 741-745.

76   *When we eat meals high in carbohydrates and sugars, it essentially damages our appetite-control cells and sends a message to our brain to consume more, even if we don't need more food at that time:* Andrews, Z.B., Liu, Z-W., Wallingford, N., Erion, D.M., Borok, E., Friedman, J.M., et al. (2008). UCP2 mediates ghrelin's action on NPY/AgRP neurons by lowering free radicals. *Nature*, *454*(7206), 846-851.

76   *Healthier (unsaturated) fats such as those found in avocados, nuts, and olive oil send the* opposite *message and signal our brain to* stop *eating:* Schwartz, G.J., Fu, J., Astarita, G., Li, X., Gaetani, S., Campolongo, P., et al. (2008). The lipid messenger OEA links dietary fat intake to satiety. *Cell Metabolism*, *8*(4), 281-288.

77   *In comparison to the broccoli group, the group that consumed one serving of peas per week for 12 months did not see significant changes in gene expression:* Traka, M., Gasper, A.V., Melchini, A., Bacon, J.R., Needs, P.W., Frost, V., et al. (2008). Broccoli consumption interacts with GSTM1 to perturb oncogenic signaling pathways in the prostate [Electronic version]. *PLoS ONE, 3*(7), e2568, 1-14.

The researchers attribute this to the difference between less nutrient-rich vegetables (e.g., peas, iceberg lettuce, and cucumbers) and cruciferous vegetables (e.g., broccoli, cauliflower, sprouts, and cabbage). Eating so-called "superfoods" like broccoli may even help you breathe easier. A study conducted by medical researchers at UCLA revealed that people who ate seven ounces of broccoli sprouts just three times a week saw up to a 200% increase in the production of proteins that make antioxidants in their nasal cells. This suggests that consuming such foods might ward off inflammation caused by allergies, pollution, or other respiratory conditions.

Champeau, R. (2009, March 2). Broccoli may help protect against respiratory conditions like asthma. Retrieved September 23, 2009, from UCLA Newsroom Web site: http:// newsroom.ucla.edu/portal/ucla/broccoli-may-help-protect-against-81667.aspx

78   *Among 400,000 Americans we surveyed in more depth, only 27% get the recommended 30 minutes or more of exercise five days per week:* Mendes, E. (2009, May 26). *In U.S., nearly half exercise less than three days a week.* Retrieved September 23, 2009, from Gallup Web site: http://www.gallup.com/poll/118570/Nearly-Half-Exercise-Less-Three-Days-Week.aspx

Amount of Weekly Exercise: A Missed Opportunity?

Percentage of Adults Aged 18 and Older

Exercise 5 Days or More Per Week (150 Minutes or More)	27%
Exercise 3-4 Days Per Week (90-120 Minutes)	24%
Exercise Less Than 3 Days Per Week (Less Than 90 Minutes)	49%

Aggregate of interviews conducted May 1, 2008-April 30, 2009
Gallup-Healthways Well-Being Index

78   *We found that each additional day of exercise in a given week —
at least up to six days when people reach a point of diminishing
returns — continues to boost energy levels:* Pelham, B.W. (2009,
November 3). *Exercise and well-being: A little goes a long way.*
Retrieved November 19, 2009, from Gallup Web site: http://
www.gallup.com/poll/124073/Exercise-Little-Goes-Long.
aspx

The Gallup-Healthways Well-Being Index revealed the extent
to which even a little exercise can go a long way. Compared
with those who say they did not exercise at all in a given week,
those who say they exercised for at least 30 minutes on one
or two days are less likely to be obese. For those who say they
exercised five or six days, the likelihood of obesity is cut nearly
in half. The results are from more than 250,000 interviews
conducted in 2009 as part of the Gallup-Healthways Well-
Being Index. Interestingly, these data suggest that exercising
seven days a week may be overkill, for both weight loss and our
overall wellbeing.

NUMBER OF DAYS OF EXERCISE IN THE PAST WEEK	PERCENTAGE OBESE
No Days	35%
1-2 Days	28%
3-4 Days	23%
5-6 Days	19%
7 Days	20%

Obesity is assessed on the basis of respondents' self-reports of their height and weight, which are then used to calculate standard body mass index (BMI) scores. Individual BMI values of 30 or above are classified as "obese."
Gallup-Healthways Well-Being Index

78   *A recent experiment revealed that just 20 minutes of exercise could improve our mood for several hours* **after** *we finish working out:* Hellmich, N. (2009, June 2). Good mood can run a long time after workout [Electronic version]. *USA TODAY.* Retrieved September 23, 2009, from http://usatoday.com

78   *Those who exercised for just 20 minutes had a significant improvement in their mood after 2, 4, 8, and 12 hours when compared to those who did not exercise:* Other studies have shown that at least 30 minutes of moderate exercise a day can have major benefits for long-term health. Regular exercise can improve good cholesterol, lower blood pressure, prevent type 2 diabetes, keep weight off, keep bones healthy, prevent certain types of cancers, strengthen the immune system, improve depression and anxiety, and help us sleep. In addition to the short-term effect of boosting our mood, exercising reduces stress and increases energy and stamina.

Mayo Clinic. (2008). Moderate exercise. *Mayo Clinic Health Letter, 26*(1), 1-3.

78-79   *On days when you don't have 20 or 30 minutes to exercise, a mere*
11 minutes of lifting weights has been shown to increase metabolic
rate, which helps you burn more fat throughout the day: Kirk,
E.P., Donnelly, J.F., Smith, B.K., Honas, J., LeCheminant,
J.D., Bailey, B.W., et al. (2009). Minimal resistance training
improves daily energy expenditure and fat oxidation. *Medicine*
& Science in Sports & Exercise, 41(5), 1122-1129.

79   *A comprehensive analysis of more than 70 trials found that*
exercising is much more effective at eliminating fatigue
than prescription drugs *used for this purpose:* Puetz, T.W.,
O'Connor, P.J., & Dishman, R.K. (2006). Effects of chronic
exercise on feelings of energy and fatigue: A quantitative
synthesis. *Psychological Bulletin, 132*(6), 866-876.

79   *One of the primary reasons people exercise regularly is because*
it makes them feel better about themselves and their appearance,
and it boosts their confidence: Krucoff, C., & Krucoff, M.
(2000). Peak performance: How a regular exercise program can
enhance sexuality and help prevent prostate cancer. *American*
Fitness, 19(6), 32-36.

Penhollow, T.M., & Young, M. (2004, October 5). Sexual
desirability and sexual performance: Does exercise and
fitness really matter? *Electronic Journal of Human Sexuality,*
7. Retrieved September 23, 2009, from http://www.ejhs.org/
volume7/fitness.html

79   *Researchers at Columbia University found that our psychological*
perceptions of our body image could be as important as objective
measures like body mass index (BMI): Muennig, P., Jia, H., Lee,
R., & Lubetkin, E. (2008). I think therefore I am: Perceived

ideal weight as a determinant of health. *American Journal of Public Health*, *98*(3), 501-506.

81   *But we're getting less sleep with each passing year, and we now sleep an average of 6.7 hours during a weeknight:* WB&A Market Research. (2009). *2009 sleep in America poll: summary of findings.* Retrieved September 23, 2009, from the National Sleep Foundation Web site: http://www.sleepfoundation.org/article/sleep-america-polls/2009-health-and-safety

82   *Scientists are discovering that we learn to remember and make connections* **more effectively when we are asleep** *than we do when we are awake:* Stickgold, R., & Wehrwein, P. (2009, April 18). Sleep now, remember later. *Newsweek.* Retrieved September 23, 2009, from http://www.newsweek.com

82   *A 2004 study illustrates the importance of sleep and how it helps our brain mentally catalog what we have learned each day:* Stickgold, R., & Ellenbogen, J.M. (2008, August). Sleep on it: How snoozing makes you smarter. *Scientific American Mind*, Retrieved September 23, 2009, from http://www.scientificamerican.com/article.cfm?id=how-snoozing-makes-you-smarter

83-84   *Short-duration sleepers were 35% more likely to experience a substantial weight gain, and long-duration sleepers were 25% more likely to have a substantial weight gain:* Chaput, J.P., Despres, J.P., Bouchard, C., & Tremblay, A. (2008). The association between sleep duration and weight gain in adults: A 6-year prospective study from the Quebec family study. *Sleep*, *31*(4), 517-523.

84   *This might be due to a hormonal imbalance — caused by a sleepless night — that actually increases our appetite the next day:* Motivala, S.J., Tomiyama, A.J., Ziegler, M., Khandrika, S., & Irwin, M.R. (2009). Nocturnal levels of ghrelin and leptin and sleep in chronic insomnia. *Psychoneuroendocrinology*, 34(4), 540-545.

84   *Over time, a lack of sleep has also been shown to increase the risk of type 2 diabetes and overall risk of death:* American Academy of Sleep Medicine (2009, June 11). Link found between poor sleep quality and increased risk of death. *ScienceDaily.* Retrieved July 10, 2009, from http://www.sciencedaily.com/releases/2009/06/090610091240.htm

University of Chicago Medical Center (2008, January 2). Lack of sleep may increase risk of type 2 diabetes. *ScienceDaily.* Retrieved December 21, 2009, from http://www.sciencedaily.com/releases/2008/01/080101093903.htm

84   *So adding even 30 minutes or an hour of sleep could help us stay healthy, including warding off the common cold:* Cohen, S., Doyle, W.J., Turner, R., Alper, C.M., & Skoner, D.P. (2003). Sociability and susceptibility to the common cold. *Psychological Science, 14*(5), 389-395.

National Heart, Lung, and Blood Institute. (2006, April). *In brief: Your guide to healthy sleep* (National Institutes of Health Publication No. 06-5800). Retrieved September 24, 2009, from http://www.nhlbi.nih.gov/health/public/sleep/healthysleepfs.htm

85   *One experiment revealed that just having a healthy option on a menu (a side salad) actually made people* three times as likely to select an unhealthy option *(a side of french fries) when compared to a menu* without *the side salad as an option:* Wilcox, K., Vallen, B., Block, L., & Fitzsimons, G.J. (2009). Vicarious goal fulfillment: When the mere presence of a healthy option leads to an ironically indulgent decision. *Journal of Consumer Research, 36*(3), 380-393.

86   *Even in a developed country like the United States, the percentages are alarmingly similar to this global average:* World Poll, based on in-person and telephone interviews with 463,933 national adults, aged 15 and older, conducted June 2005-October 2009. For results based on this sample, one can say with 95% confidence that the margin of error is ±0.1 percentage points. For individual countries with annual sample sizes of 1,000, the 95% margin of error is ±3.1 percentage points.

Gallup-Healthways Well-Being Index, based on landline and cell phone interviews with more than 700,000 national adults, aged 18 and older, conducted January 2, 2008-December 30, 2009. For results based on this sample, one can say with 95% confidence that the margin of error is ±0.2 percentage points.

86   *For example, in the United States, healthcare costs represent 16% of the total economy and are projected to reach 20% of the nation's Gross Domestic Product (GDP) in the next decade:* U.S. Department of Health and Human Services. (2009, November 17). Statement by Kathleen Sebelius, Secretary, U.S. Department of Health and Human Services, on FY 2010 budget before Committee on Appropriations, Subcommittee

on Labor, Health and Human Services, Education, and related Agencies. Retrieved November 23, 2009, from http://www. hhs.gov/asl/testify/2009/06/t20090609b.html

86   *In 1999, the cost of insuring a family in the United States was approximately $5,700. As of 2009, that cost has soared to more than $13,000, and according to projections, it will reach nearly $25,000 by 2018:* Kaiser Family Foundation and the Health Research & Educational Trust. (2009). *Employer health benefits 2009 annual survey.* Retrieved November 19, 2009, from http:// ehbs.kff.org/pdf/2009/7936.pdf

Congressional Budget Office. (2008, February 29). *Taxes and health insurance: Presentation to the tax policy center and the American tax policy institute.* Retrieved November 19, 2009, from http://www.cbo.gov/ftpdocs/90xx/doc9009/02.29.2008- Taxes_and_Health_Insurance.pdf

86-87   *Two out of three U.S. residents report having problems with medical bills, going without needed care, being underinsured, or living completely uninsured as a result of these soaring costs:* The Commonwealth Fund: A Private Foundation Working Toward a High Performance Health System. (2008, August 20). *Losing ground: How the loss of adequate health insurance is burdening working families — findings from the Commonwealth Fund biennial health insurance surveys, 2001-2007.* Retrieved December 27, 2009, from http://www.commonwealthfund. org/Content/Publications/Fund-Reports/2008/Aug/Losing- Ground--How-the-Loss-of-Adequate-Health-Insurance-Is- Burdening-Working-Families--8212-Finding.aspx

87   *According to a Harvard study, in 2007, 62% of all personal*
        bankruptcies in the United States had a medical cause:
        Himmelstein, D.U., Thorne, D., Warren, E., & Woolhandler,
        S. (2009). Medical bankruptcy in the United States, 2007:
        Results of a national study. *The American Journal of Medicine,*
        122(8),741-746.

87   *As a result of how this system works, estimates show that each*
        healthy American is paying a tax of an additional $1,464
        per year because of colleagues who lead less healthy lifestyles:
        Thompson, D., Brown, J.B., Nichols, G.A., Elmer, P.J., &
        Oster, G. (2001). Body mass index and future healthcare costs:
        A retrospective cohort study. *Obesity Research, 9*(3), 210-218.

        Centers for Medicare & Medicaid Services. (2009).
        National health expenditure projections 2008-2018: Forecast
        summary and selected tables. Retrieved January 8, 2010, from
        http://www.cms.hhs.gov/nationalhealthexpenddata/03_
        nationalhealthaccountsprojected.asp

87   *Other studies have found that* **more than half** *of all healthcare*
        spending in the United States is consumed by just 5% of the
        population: Berk, M.L., & Monheit, A.C. (1992). The
        concentration of health expenditures: An update. *Health Affairs,*
        11(4), 145-149.

87   *Further, 75% of medical costs are due to largely preventable*
        conditions (stress, tobacco use, physical inactivity, and poor food
        choices): Roizen, M. (Speaker). (n.d.). *Improving well-being*
        through behavior change (Video). Washington, D.C.: Gallup,
        Inc., and Healthways.

88   *Researchers studying type 2 diabetes, for example, found that by putting people on a healthier diet, they could significantly reduce glucose, triglycerides, and cholesterol, while decreasing the use of prescription medications by 43% — in just 4½ months:* Barnard, N.D., Cohen, J., Jenkins, D.J.A., Turner-McGrievy, G., Gloede, L., Jaster, B., et al. (2006). A low-fat, vegan diet improves glycemic control and cardiovascular risk factors in a randomized clinical trial in individuals with type 2 diabetes. *Diabetes Care*, 29(8), 1777-1783.

5: Community Wellbeing

94   *In the United States, residents of several cities have serious concerns about safety, air pollution, and other environmental contaminants. When these needs aren't met, it is difficult to have thriving wellbeing:* World Poll, based on in-person and telephone interviews with 463,933 national adults, aged 15 and older, conducted June 2005-October 2009. For results based on this sample, one can say with 95% confidence that the margin of error is ±0.1 percentage points. For individual countries with annual sample sizes of 1,000, the 95% margin of error is ±3.1 percentage points.

Gallup-Healthways Well-Being Index, based on landline and cell phone interviews with more than 700,000 national adults, aged 18 and older, conducted January 2, 2008-December 30, 2009. For results based on this sample, one can say with 95% confidence that the margin of error is ±0.2 percentage points.

Gallup and John S. and James L. Knight Foundation. (n.d.) *Soul of the community overall report*. Retrieved September 24, 2009, from http://www.soulofthecommunity.org/node/64

Saad, L. (2009, May 25). *Water pollution Americans' top green concern*. Retrieved November 20, 2009, from Gallup Web site: http://www.gallup.com/poll/117079/Water-Pollution-Americans-Top-Green-Concern.aspx

94   *While the things that make a community "perfect" will be different for everyone, people use common themes to describe ideal communities:* Gallup and John S. and James L. Knight Foundation. (n.d.) *Soul of the community overall report.* Retrieved September 24, 2009, from http://www.soulofthecommunity.org

For a listing of some of the U.S. cities that have residents with the highest levels of wellbeing, see Appendix F: Wellbeing Across the United States.

96   *People reported experiencing increased moods* **before** *and* **after** *they donated blood:* What's more, those who had donated four or more times had much lower levels of nervousness beforehand, higher expectations of good feelings, and a stronger commitment to continue donation.

Piliavin, J.A. (2003). Doing well by doing good: Benefits for the benefactor. In C.L.M. Keyes & J. Haidt (Eds.), *Flourishing: Positive psychology and the life well-lived* (pp. 227-247). Washington, D.C.: American Psychological Association.

97   *According to Jordan Grafman, a neuroscientist at the National Institutes of Health, these reactions in the brain "help us plan into the future, feel emotionally closer to others, and give us a sense of reward after a behavior — which reinforces that behavior, making it more likely we will do the same thing again":* Stoddard, G. (2009, July/August). What we get from giving. *Men's Health, 24*(6), 108-115.

97   *This might explain why some volunteers get a "helper's high"* *— they feel stronger, more energetic, and more motivated after* *helping others even in the smallest ways:* Stoddard, G. (2009, July/August). What we get from giving. *Men's Health, 24*(6), 108-115.

97   *When we do things for others, we see how we can make a* *difference, and this gives us confidence in our own ability to* *create change:* One study revealed that adolescents who get involved in volunteering have higher future aspirations, higher self-esteem, and increased motivation toward schoolwork.

     Johnson, M.K., Beebe, T., Mortimer, J.T., & Snyder, M. (1998). Volunteerism in adolescence: A process perspective. *Journal of Research on Adolescence, 8*(3), 309-332.

97   *Throughout the course of our lives, well-doing promotes deeper* *social interaction, enhanced meaning and purpose, and a more* *active lifestyle — while keeping us from being too preoccupied* *with ourselves or getting into harmful emotional states:* Pang, S. (2009, May 22). Is altruism good for the altruistic giver? *Dartmouth Undergraduate Journal of Science.* Retrieved September 28, 2009, from http://dujs.dartmouth.edu/ spring-2009/is-altruism-good-for-the-altruistic-giver

97-98   *Several studies have shown a link between altruistic behavior* *and increases in overall longevity, and researchers have speculated* *that this might be due in part to how* **well-doing inoculates us** **against stress and negative emotions**: As Harvard political scientist Robert Putnam described, "If you belong to no groups but decide to join one, you cut your risk of dying over the next year *in half*." Our involvement in community groups might also provide a buffer against memory loss that occurs with age. A six-year longitudinal study of 16,638 elderly people revealed that the least social people experienced more rapid memory loss as they aged. However, among those who were the most socially active, memory declined at *less than half* the rate that it did for the least social people.

Ertel, K.A., Glymour, M.M., & Berkman, L.F. (2008). Effects of social integration on preserving memory function in a nationally representative US elderly population. *American Journal of Public Health, 98*(7), 1215-1220.

Putnam, R.D. (2000). *Bowling alone.* New York: Simon & Schuster.

98   *Even in the case of something as significant as donating your organs, your decision is heavily influenced by whether the system is set up to opt you in or to opt you out:* Johnson, E.J., & Goldstein, D. (2003, November 21). Do defaults save lives? *Science, 302,* 1338-1339.

100   *In China, for example, more than 1 million people are reported to be in need of organ donations, yet only 1% actually receive the transplant surgery they need. Because of the nation's organ shortage, four in five people die while waiting for a transplant:* Juan, S. (2009, September 17). Four in five die in waiting for organ donation. *China Daily.* Retrieved November 20, 2009, from   http://www.chinadaily.com.cn/china/2009-09/17/content_8702813.htm

103   *But if you enroll in the program* **with three friends or colleagues you already know,** *the odds of maintaining your weight loss go up to 66%:* Wing, R.R., & Jeffery, R.W. (1999). Benefits

of recruiting participants with friends and increasing social support for weight loss and maintenance. *Journal of Consulting and Clinical Psychology, 67*(1), 132-138.

Concluding Thoughts: Measuring What Makes Life Worthwhile

109 *As Bobby Kennedy said just a few months before his death in 1968, we continue to gauge the progress of our lives, our organizations, and our communities based on narrow and shallow measures:* John F. Kennedy Presidential Library & Museum. (n.d.). *Quotations of Robert F. Kennedy.* Retrieved September 1, 2009, from http://www.jfklibrary. org/Historical+Resources/Archives/Reference+Desk/ Quotations+of+Robert+F.+Kennedy.htm

110 *As Nobel Prize-winning economist Thomas Schelling described, we behave as if we're two different people: one who wants a lean body and another who wants dessert:* Schelling, T.C. (1978). Egonomics, or the art of self-management. *The American Economic Review, 68*(2), 290-294.

110-111 *An extra half-hour of sleep or an extra hour of social time can be the difference between a great day and a mediocre day:* The difference in hours of sleep between a good day and a bad day is surprisingly low. During good days, people spent an average of 7.1 hours sleeping the night before. Those who had bad days averaged 6.6 hours. Social time is another strong predictor of good versus bad days. People who had good days averaged 1.4 more hours of social time than those who had bad days.

B: Daily Wellbeing: How We Spend Our Time

125 *Recently, a team that included three of Gallup's senior scientists... proposed a formal approach dubbed National Time Accounting for measuring how we use our time:* Krueger, A.B., Kahneman, D., Schkade, D., Schwarz, N., & Stone, A.A. (2008). *National time accounting: The currency of life.* Princeton, NJ: Princeton University, Department of Economics, Industrial Relations Section.

130 *Even when comparing people with identical incomes, TV owners around the world still enjoy higher levels of wellbeing and optimism:* Pelham, B. (2008, March 31). *TV ownership may be good for well-being.* Retrieved December 23, 2009, from Gallup Web site: http://www.gallup.com/poll/105850/Ownership-May-Good-WellBeing.aspx

C: Increasing Wellbeing in Organizations: The Role of Managers and Leaders

134 *This type of progressive thinking is not uncommon among the best leaders we interviewed, as they often consider the broader influence they have on their followers and the networks that surround them:* Rath, T., & Conchie, B. (2008). *Strengths based leadership: Great leaders, teams, and why people follow.* New York: Gallup Press.

134 *Mervyn Davies, the former chairman of Standard Chartered Bank, described how he helped more than 70,000 bank employees (across 70 countries) know that the organization cared about their personal lives:* Rath, T., & Conchie, B. (2008). *Strengths based leadership: Great leaders, teams, and why people follow.* New York: Gallup Press.

D: Technical Report: The Research and Development of Gallup's Wellbeing Metrics

138   *In 1960, Dr. Gallup published a study and subsequent book titled* The Secrets of a Long Life: Gallup, G., & Hill, E. (1960). *The secrets of a long life.* New York: Bernard Geis.

140   *Nobel laureate Daniel Kahneman and University of Illinois at Urbana-Champaign psychology professor Ed Diener have been influential in conceiving the contemporary views of wellbeing:* Kahneman, D., Diener, E., & Schwarz, N. (Eds.). (1998). *Wellbeing: The foundations of hedonic psychology.* New York: Russell Sage Foundation.

140-141 *In the journal article "Guidelines for National Indicators of Subjective Well-Being and Ill-Being," Diener defines subjective wellbeing as "all of the various types of evaluations, both positive and negative, that people make of their lives. . . .":* Diener, E. (2005). Guidelines for national indicators of subjective well-being and ill-being. *Journal of Happiness Studies, 7,* 397-404.

141   *Similarly, in the book* The Science of Well-Being: Integrating Neurobiology, Psychology, and Social Science, *Kahneman makes note of the distinction between "experienced well-being" and "evaluative well-being":* Kahneman, D., & Riis, J. (2005). Living and thinking about it: Two perspectives on life. In F. Huppert, N. Baylis, & B. Kaverne (Eds.), *The science of wellbeing: Integrating neurobiology, psychology, and social science* (pp. 285-304). Oxford, United Kingdom: Oxford University Press.

141   *Inspired by the work of Kahneman and his colleagues, the Gallup global study adapted these methods to a large-scale survey environment by framing a series of experience and emotion questions within the context of the past 24 hours:* The Gallup Organization. (2007). *The state of global well-being.* New York: Author.

144   Life Evaluation: Present *(0-10 scale);* Life Evaluation: Future *(0-10 scale):* Cantril, H. (1965). *The pattern of human concerns.* New Brunswick, NJ: Rutgers University Press.

F: Wellbeing Across the United States

169   *Percentages of residents who are "thriving," "struggling," and "suffering" for states and cities (in the United States) were derived based on how people evaluated their lives on the Cantril Self-Anchoring Striving Scale:* Cantril, H. (1965). *The pattern of human concerns.* New Brunswick, NJ: Rutgers University Press.

Acknowledgements

Wellbeing: The Five Essential Elements is the product of decades of work conducted by our colleagues at Gallup, leading scientists from the academic community, and millions of interviews from around the world. While we extracted many of the key findings in the preceding pages, the book itself is just one piece of a much larger production led by the following teams:

Executive Publishers
Jim Clifton, Larry Emond, Piotr Juszkiewicz

Editors
Geoff Brewer, Kelly Henry, Trista Kunce

Project Leaders
Jeff Jokerst, Emily Meyer, Jessica Tyler

Research Director
Sangeeta Agrawal

Scientific Advisors for Global Research
Angus Deaton, Ed Diener, Daniel Kahneman, Alan Krueger, Gale Muller, Arthur Stone

Graphic Designers
Samantha Allemang, Chin-Yee Lai, Seth Warrick

Technology Experts
Asen Asenov, Beau Braig, Dan Cihal, Elizabeth Davies, Swati Jain, Kate Johansson, Matt Johnson, Billy Krasso, Brandon Mueller, Courage Noko, Vishal Santoshi, Keerat Sharma, Ramzi Yassine

Publishing Team

Ashly Beaman, Bette Curd, Julie Curd, Dan Draus, Barbara Henricks, Julie Lamski, Ron Newman, Eric Nielsen, Mark Rupprecht, Mary Samson, Yvonne Sen, Pat Sterba, Mindy Wells, Alan Woods

Global Research Leadership

Jeff Bechtolt, Richard Burkholder, Marc Carpenter, Jon Clifton, Tim Dean, Christine Delmeiren, Cynthia English, Neli Esipova, Jihad Fakhreddine, Johanna Godoy, Tim Gravelle, Stephanie Hatfield, Agnes Illyes, Robert Manchin, Jenny Marlar, Ed Muller, Nicole Naurath, Glenn Phelps, Anita Pugliese, Jesus Rios, Rajesh Srinivasan, Darby Miller Steiger, Bob Tortora

Editorial Advisors

Jim Asplund, Justin Bibb, Nikki Blacksmith, Shelly Blakeman, TJ Bolt, Scot Caldwell, Jody Delichte, Alan DeMuro, Wendy Dowd, Libby Engelbart, Ryan Feagan, John Fleming, Christie Fraser, Tonya Fredstrom, Frank Fritsch, Keri Garman, Suz Graf, Andrew Green, Carleen Haas, Julie Hahn, John Harris, RaLinda Harter, Lisette Islas, Susan Jones, Eric Kettunen, Jason Krieger, Rob Kroenert, Michelle Krogmeier, Mark Lane, Shane Lopez, Allison Lowry, Jennifer Mellein, Jane Miller, Lymari Morales, Melissa Moreno, Helen Musura, Tom Nolan, Ed O'Boyle, David Ouimet, Maggie Ozan, Rachel Penrod, John Pruitt, Ashley Rath, Connie Rath, Keith Roberts, Leslie Roberts, Ken Royal, Jeannie Ruhlman, Tony Rutigliano, Rani Salman, Ken Shearer, Jennifer Silva, Kelly Slater, Matt Stencil, Sonja Taber, Shari Theer, Ray Vigil, Rodd Wagner, Al Winseman, Warren Wright

Perhaps most importantly, we would like to thank the thousands of Gallup interviewers around the world and all of the individuals who have taken the time to participate in our research. As we mentioned throughout the book, the things that we learned from these world citizens were what enabled us to uncover the common elements of wellbeing.

About the Authors

Tom Rath

Tom Rath has written three international bestsellers in the last decade. His first book, *How Full Is Your Bucket?*, was a #1 *New York Times* bestseller. Rath's book *StrengthsFinder 2.0* is a long-running #1 *Wall Street Journal* bestseller and was listed by *USA TODAY* as the top-selling business book of 2008. His latest bestseller, *Strengths Based Leadership*, was published in 2009. In total, Rath's books have sold more than 2 million copies in the U.S. alone and have made more than 100 appearances on the *Wall Street Journal* bestseller list.

Rath has been with Gallup for 14 years and currently leads Gallup's workplace research and leadership consulting around the world. Rath also serves on the board of VHL.org, an organization dedicated to cancer research and patient support. He earned degrees from the University of Michigan and the University of Pennsylvania. Tom and his wife, Ashley, and their daughter, Harper, live in Washington, D.C.

Jim Harter, Ph.D.

Jim Harter is Chief Scientist for Gallup's international workplace management and wellbeing practices. He coauthored the *New York Times* bestseller *12: The Elements of Great Managing*, which is based on the largest worldwide study of employee engagement. Since joining Gallup in 1985, Harter has authored or coauthored more than 1,000 research studies, some of which have been reported on in bestselling management books, academic articles, book chapters, and publications such as *The Wall Street Journal*, *The New York Times*, and *USA TODAY*. He is coauthor of "Manage Your Human Sigma," published in the *Harvard Business Review*. Harter earned his doctorate in psychological and cultural studies at the University of Nebraska-Lincoln. Jim and his wife, RaLinda, and their sons, Joey and Sam, live in Omaha, Nebraska.